DO YOU REMEMBER

# Elvis Presley?

THE LIFE AND TIMES OF THE KING OF ROCK & ROLL

DO YOU REMEMBER

# Elvis Presley?

## THE LIFE AND TIMES OF THE KING OF ROCK & ROLL

CHRIS EDWARDS

BLUE
RIVER
PRESS

INDIANAPOLIS, INDIANA

Do You Remember Elvis Presley? The Life and Times of the King of Rock & Roll
Copyright © 2024 by Chris Edwards

Published by Blue River Press
Indianapolis, Indiana
www.brpressbooks.com

Distributed by Cardinal Publishers Group
A Tom Doherty Company, Inc.
www.cardinalpub.com

ISBN: 978-1-68157-235-2

Book Design: Tessa Gunderman
Editor: Tessa Gunderman

Printed in the United States of America

10 9 8 7 6 5 4 3 2 1    24 25 26 27 28 29 30

# Table of Contents

# Chapter One

---

# Tupelo, Mississippi

It's June 26, 1977; Elvis Presley stood before a crowd of 18,000 at Market Square Arena in Indianapolis and sang his last song. Throughout the evening, Elvis struggled to remember lyrics and often slurred his words while speaking to the audience. He sometimes drifted off mid-sentence only to suddenly snap back with a cockeyed grin and a quick joke. Some music critics thought that Elvis' performance on that summer night, like so many of his shows over the past three years, made a mockery of a man once considered the greatest performer of his era. All of this might have been true, but when Elvis twisted the gaudy rings on his fingers, adjusted the strap on his guitar, and crooned "Are You Lonesome Tonight?" he reminded the audience of what he had once been: a man whose hips shook the foundations of a generation's culture and whose voice pulled at a generation of hearts.

Not long after that last song, Elvis exited the stage. He intended to take a break at his home in Graceland and spend some time with his daughter. About three weeks later, special news bulletins across all the major networks broke the news of Elvis Presley's death. It shocked the American public into a collective state of grieving nostalgia. For two and a half decades, from the time that a teenaged Elvis made a hit single out of an old rhythm and blues song called "That's All Right, Mama," right up until his last lonesome song, Elvis reigned as the king of rock n' roll.

As crowds of mourners filled the streets around Elvis' mansion at Graceland, in Memphis Tennessee they remembered a man who had electrified the culture on *The Ed Sullivan Show*, answered Uncle Sam's call to join the Army, and lit up a countless number of drive-in screens with his films. They remembered how he looked in that tight black leather suit when he performed his comeback special, and the way that he remade Las Vegas with his nightly acts. They remembered, too, how Elvis failed to emotionally recover from the untimely death of his beloved mother, and the way that he turned to the pills as a way of assuaging his grief. They remembered the way Elvis' manager, Colonel Tom Parker, lurked in the background of his life. When adoring fans remember Elvis Presley, they remembered a man who came from the humblest of origins.

On January 8, 1935, during the hardest of hard times, Elvis Aaron Presley was born right along with tragedy. Elvis' mother, Gladys, just twenty-three years old, gave birth to a son named Jesse Garon but the baby died during the labor. Jesse's twin, Elvis, came into the world just a little while later. Gladys held the surviving boy all the more tightly and believed then and for the rest of her days that Jesse's strength entered into Elvis.

Shown: Elvis' birthplace, designated as a historic land-mark by the state of Mississippi. You can tour it and many other exhibits at the Elvis Birthplace & Museum in Tupelo, MS.

The Great Depression hit the whole country but few places felt the effects more severely than Tupelo, Mississippi, where Gladys and her husband, Vernon Presley, lived the best they could in a two-room shack. In 1935, in a place like Tupelo, and with a living son to care for, there was little time to mourn even the death of a baby. Vernon placed the little body of Jesse Garon in a shoebox.

Then he dug a hole in a backcountry graveyard and placed the shoebox at the bottom. Little Elvis, squirming in his makeshift crib, needed care. Life had to move on.

Like just about everybody else at the time, Vernon and Gladys tried to scrounge a dollar wherever one could be found. Vernon worked here and there as a day laborer, but Tupelo, Mississippi in the 1930's was not the best place to find employment. Elvis Presley grew up with uncertainty and poverty, but he seemed not to know it. Elvis grew up like just about every other southern country boy, hunting, fishing, and roughhousing on the school playground.

On Sundays, Elvis attended Pentecostal Church services with Gladys and Vernon. The Pentecostals quivered with faith and shouted the glory of Jesus during services. A Pentecostal preacher didn't deliver a sermon, he performed it, and the congregation responded with shouts of praise that came from the belly. A southern preacher in that time emoted from behind the pulpit, in front of the pulpit, and sometimes out into the crowd. It wasn't a good sermon unless the parishioners got up and swayed along with the rhythm of the faith.

The first decade of Elvis' life represented some of the most important years in American history. Through the radio, the Presley family would have heard news as well as music, and the big events of Elvis' childhood years would create social conditions that would eventually make him into a star.

Three years before Elvis' birth, in 1932, Franklin Delano Roosevelt had been elected by promising Americans a New Deal during the Depression. Radios were a feature of most households by that time, and Mr. Roosevelt spoke directly into American homes with his "fireside chats," starting in the spring of 1933. For many, Roosevelt was a real and comforting presence during those uncertain times. Those radio broadcasts created an intimacy with the presidency that had never existed before, and the welfare checks sent to the unemployed connected daily family life with the government in a way that no previous generation had ever conceived of.

Prior to Roosevelt's election, most black Americans voted Republican because that was "The Party of Lincoln." New Deal assistance checks went out to black families as well as white families and that had a deep effect on black voters who came out in huge numbers to help elect Mr. Roosevelt four times. Elvis grew up in a largely black area of Mississippi, with black friends, neighbors, and culture. FDR was the only president he knew for the first ten years of his life, and the racial fairness of the New Deal had a deep effect on how Elvis saw himself, his fellow black Americans, and his country.

Throughout the late 1930's, many Americans hoped that the United States could stay out of the political problems afflicting East Asia and Europe, where imperialist Japan and Nazi Germany militarized and invaded their neighbors. However, after the Japanese bombed an American naval base at Pearl Harbor, Hawaii, President Roosevelt declared that December 7, 1941, the day of the attack, would be "a day that will live in infamy." The United States went to war with both Japan and Germany.

Such large-scale historical events must have seemed quite distant from Tupelo, Mississippi, but they would have an important effect on the life of Elvis Presley. The iron curtain that divided Europe would have to be guarded, in large part, by American troops. The Cold War in Europe would keep the United States on a war footing and ensure the continuance of the army draft. The Japanese defeat in Asia, would lead to a Communist takeover of China. Fear of the Communist threat in the Korean Peninsula and in Southeast Asia would drive U.S. foreign policy, and the Korean War and Vietnamese conflict would define Elvis' generation.

The nuclear age began in 1945 when the United States dropped two atomic bombs on Japanese cities and forced the Empire of the Rising Sun to surrender. The atomic bombs possessed such destructive power, that everyone understood that humanity had entered into a new era. That same year, another type of high-energy production was in its earliest developmental phase. A ten-year-old Elvis Presley made his performance debut at the Mississippi-Alabama Fair and Dairy Show. Still too short to reach the microphone, he had to stand on a chair. He crooned a tear-jerker, "Old Shep" about a boy and his beloved pet dog.

Elvis' parents were eager to support their son's musical talent, but at the time Elvis was more interested in hunting. With his eleventh birthday approaching, he kept pestering his mother for a rifle.

Elvis and father, Vernon, mother Gladys, moved from Tupelo, MS to Memphis, TN in 1948.

Instead, Gladys went to the local hardware store and splurged on a guitar. Although disappointed at first, Elvis soon became infatuated with his new instrument. He would play anywhere he could find an audience, even at school, and learned how to time his voice with the guitar's music.

Apparently, Elvis couldn't win over everyone. Some of the boys at school snatched the guitar, and sliced the strings so that Elvis could not play. This didn't stop Elvis for long as he continued to strum the guitar and fine-tune his singing as puberty deepened his voice. By the time he was fourteen, Elvis was the greatest show on his parents' front porch.

It was time, however, for the Presleys to move. By 1949, the Great Depression had ended for most of the country but Tupelo, Mississippi remained dirt poor and job prospects were few. Vernon decided to move north, to Memphis, Tennessee, in search of better opportunities. Elvis would go to high school in one of the great musical centers of the world. He would slick his hair back and learn to wail his lyrics and strum his guitar in a place where jazz, country music, and the blues all came together to create a whole new genre of music, complete with a culture of youthful rebellion. The name for this movement was Rock n' Roll.

## Chapter Two

# Sun Records

Sam Phillips, the owner of the Memphis-based Sun Studio and Records, was born in early 1923 and grew up picking cotton on his daddy's farm in hard-scrabble rural Alabama. Phillips worked shoulder-to-shoulder with black laborers. Those black field workers sang songs with rhythms that originated in West Africa. Those songs sustained millions of their ancestors through the long and brutal period of American slavery. There in those sun-drenched southern cotton fields, a young Phillips learned about how music could move people.

Phillips first came to Memphis, Tennessee when he was just sixteen. The family had been passing through on a trip and Phillips snuck away to see Beale Street, where black musicians had created the blues. There, in a city where a new musical culture gestated, Phillips felt an immediate sense of belonging. He had to leave with his family, but Phillips promised himself he would return one day.

Just before Phillips graduated high school, his father died. Phillips's mother and aunt needed financial support, so he took a job at a funeral parlor and then eventually a radio station. It was while working at the station, age nineteen, that Sam met a high-school girl named Becky Kitchen, who had shown up to play music with her sister. Sam smiled in Becky's direction, and the two soon fell in love. The youngsters married the next year, in 1943.

Sam continued to work at the radio station. At that time, most radio stations featured live musical acts. Sam and his station welcomed both white and black performers. In 1945, Sam fulfilled his dream of moving to Memphis. He got a job working for radio station WREC as an announcer. Sam and Becky moved to the music capital of the south, and Sam developed a plan to capture and package the sounds and rhythms of Beale Street. He dreamed of opening a recording studio.

On his twenty-seventh birthday, on January 3, 1950, Sam Phillips made the Memphis Recording Service open to musicians, and the Sam Phillips label, started in 1952, would go by Sun Records. Ever since his cotton-picking days in Alabama, Sam had seen music as a means of racial reconciliation. The music, not the skin color of the musicians, is what mattered. He would welcome any acts that had talent.

Sam Phillips lived out the remaining years of his twenties by recording that unique Memphis sound, the blues. This was his passion, but it didn't always pay the bills. Sam had to use his recording talents at weddings and other events in order to make money, all the while hoping that a market would open for the music he loved to record and the talent he hoped to develop.

Since the end of WWII, American music had been dominated by "crooners" who sang love ballads. The most up-tempo sound that could be found on the airwaves came in the form of big-band swing, a sound dominated by trumpets and violins. The music had no back-beat, no dancing rhythm. To find that, one had to venture down Beale Street, a place where most of white America would not go. Nor, it was thought, would white Americans tolerate a black entertainer performing on the big weekend musical variety shows.

While Sam Philips set up both his life and his recording studio in Memphis, Elvis Presley was attending L.C. Humes High School in

Sun was the first label to record Elvis Presley, Charlie Rich, Roy Orbison, Jerry Lee Lewis, Carl Perkins, and Johnny Cash.

Memphis. The Presley family was notable in Memphis for only having one child, a rarity at the time, and Vernon and Glady doted on Elvis to the point where the family sometimes shut other people out. Elvis was the epitome of a southern mama's boy and never spent the night at the houses of his friends.

When the family moved up from Tupelo, Gladys even walked Elvis part of the way to school. Then Elvis made some friends and started to pull away a little bit from his folks. His teachers described him as shy but personable, and not necessarily attracted to academics. In tenth grade, Elvis joined the ROTC and helped out in the library. By that time, his mother had found work serving coffee in a Memphis cafeteria. Elvis spent much of his free time making arts and crafts for her while at school.

Once Elvis made friends in the neighborhood, he spent his time roughhousing in pick-up football games, riding his bike around town, and catching movies. To earn money in the summers, he and his buddies mowed lawns. Elvis became more reserved during his early high school years in Memphis. In Tupelo, Elvis took his guitar to school and played songs during breaks. He didn't show off or perform like that in Memphis; he kept his musical talents more to himself.

Music meant a lot to that generation of kids since radios were smaller and cheaper after WWII ended. It was no longer the case that the family room would be taken up by one big radio that was controlled by the parents. Now teenagers could sneak off to their rooms at night and listen to hip new music, much of it played by or inspired by black musicians. For the first time, teenagers created a secret world of their own. This included Elvis, who spent many nights listening to the new Memphis sounds. Through the same radio, Elvis could also hear an up-tempo version of country, or hillbilly, music that would become known as "rockabilly" and some enthusiastic Baptist preaching.

Like a lot of mama's boys, Elvis turned shy and awkward around groups of young men. Although he played football with his neighborhood friends, Elvis never seemed to adopt the rough manners so typical of high school boys when they form into groups. Everyone in his family noticed that Elvis simply preferred the company of women; he would blossom if he was the only boy in a room of girls. Somehow his personality connected with young women; he seemed to love them all. The older ladies thought he was a sweet boy, and the younger ladies were attracted to his lanky frame, good looks, and obvious musical talents.

At sixteen, it was time for Elvis to get his first real summer job. His uncles got him on at a place in the city called Precision Tool. However, he had to go back to mowing lawns with his buddies when a safety inspector found out that Elvis was too young for the work. Elvis let his hair grow long that summer, a sign of mild rebellion in those years where young men generally hopped into a barber's chair to have their hair shorn into a flattop.

When school started up again in the Fall, Elvis uncharacteristically tried out for the football team. His teammates were less than understanding about Elvis' long hair and bullied him about it in the locker rooms. Rather than cut his locks, Elvis quit the team and spent his after-school hours wandering Beale Street, looking through shop windows and admiring the fancy cars.

In the 1950's, Beale Street may have been the most integrated place in the country. Blacks and whites passed each other on the streets, and the music had long ago gotten all mixed together. However, black folks knew that if a black person committed a crime against a white person, then they could expect to feel the full force of whites-only legal establishment. Whites knew that the opposite was not true, and while black people did technically have recourse to the law, the scales of justice were not equally balanced.

Elvis was just a kid, though, and not particularly interested in social issues. He wanted to watch movies, listen to music, play music, and dress in the latest fashions. He had been around black people his whole life, in some ways he had been immersed in black culture, and didn't think much about issues involving integration.

The Presley family remained regular church-goers, and Elvis seemed to like gospel music as much as any other kind. He watched the singers sway, felt the joy radiate from their voices, and felt the power of his religion through song. When he hung out with friends on weekends, he would typically bring his guitar and put on solo performances. He got the reputation as a show-off. He went steady with a girl who broke up with him for a young sailor, and generally spent his high school years life like everybody else.

Elvis in 1954 not long after he graduated Humes High School in the spring of 1953.

The 1950's was the first decade where it became normal for young people to finish high school, and this meant that many seventeen and eighteen year olds started working a more-or-less full time job while also going to school. His senior year, Elvis got a job assembling furniture at a plant downtown. Elvis slept through much of the school day, until his mother made him quit his job and focus on his studies.

Something transformed in Elvis during his senior year; he affected the dress and attitude of a Hollywood star. He'd come to class in a white coat and ascot tie, wearing dress pants instead of the ubiquitous teenage-boy outfit of a t-shirt and blue jeans. His school chums didn't know what to make of him. He kept a comb on him, and often ran it through all that greasy hair. He passed all of his classes but one. The record shows that Elvis Presley got an F in music.

Elvis was a member of that fortuitous generation of kids from the era who narrowly avoided being drafted off to war. The Korean

War entered a ceasefire in 1953, just as Elvis graduated high school in June of that year. Less than a month later, Elvis took a job working as a factory machinist but kept on dreaming about making music for a living. That dream brought him to Sam Philips and Sun Records.

Philips produced his first hit in the summer of 1953 with a song called "Just Walkin' in the Rain" by a group called The Prisonaires (so-called because they formed their band in a Tennessee penitentiary). Elvis drove by the Sun Records studio frequently on his forays through Memphis. That summer in 1953, Elvis went back to work at Precision Tool, and this time he was old enough to stay employed. But the assembly line work didn't fulfill Elvis, so he decided to cut a record and see what would happen.

Performers could pay a fee to have a recording made; in those days a recording came in the form of a two-side acetate record. To "cut" a record meant to carve little grooves on the edges of the acetate plate. When placed on a record-player, the plate spun in a circle and listeners had to carefully place a needle on the grooves to make the music come out. It still seemed like a magical process.

Elvis paid nearly four dollars to record his singing but what he was really doing was paying for the opportunity to audition for Mr. Phillips. Elvis could pay for a personal recording of his own music, but if Sam Phillips thought Elvis had talent, then Sun Records would distribute Elvis' songs and pay out a royalty. It would then be up to local disc jockeys (DJ's), and the general public to decide whether or not a song became a hit and a singer became a star.

Elvis started out with Frank Sinatra style ballads, which were still all the rage on the radio. While his voice was strong, nothing really grabbed the attention of Sam Phillips (or his wife, who acted as a de facto talent scout.) Sam liked Elvis though, and said he might call Elvis back to cut a record for local release. Phillips asked his secretary to make a note about this talented young man.

It was the next summer, June of 1954, when Phillips called Elvis in to record a ballad titled "Without You." Despite the obvious strength in Elvis' signing voice, the song came out flat. Phillips thought maybe Elvis would do better if he had a strong band behind him, and made introductions between Elvis, a bass player named Bill Black, and a guitarist named Scotty Moore.

Colonel Tom Parker began his career in the music industry as a promoter in 1938. By 1956 he became the manager of Elvis Presley.

On July 5, 1954, Elvis and his new band entered the Sun Records studio and labored through a few more ballads. Disappointed and a little tired, they all took a break. At that point, Elvis picked up a guitar and began to sing a Delata Blues song, called "That's All Right, Mama" by the black artist Arthur "Big Boy" Crudup. Elvis started bouncing around and singing, his hair whipping around on his forehead, just having fun with the song. Bill Black and Scotty Moore started to play along.

Sam Phillips, who had been messing with the equipment, heard the music and looked down at the boys through the recording studio window. He poked his head out the side and asked what they were all doing. The boys said they didn't really know; they were just having fun.

Sam Phillips told them to do it again, and this time he recorded it.

## Chapter Three

# Rebel Without a Cause

After the war ended in 1945, the United States started testing even more powerful atomic weapons in the remote South Pacific island region known as Bikini Atoll. The tests, at a time when the U.S. could boast to be the only country in the world with atomic weapons, garnered a lot of press attention. In 1946, French swimsuit designers named Heim and Reard named their racy new two-piece outfit after the U.S. nuclear test site. The "bikini" smirked the designers, would go off like a bomb when it hit the beaches. A new era of sexual liberation, marked by changes in music, movies, and social attitudes, seemed to be emerging. Babies, and there were a lot of them, born in the United States between 1946 and 1965 were part of a baby boom generation.

After 1946, Americans got used to growing levels prosperity. Soldiers returning from the war tended to have some "Government Issue" (G.I.) money, and they bought small but solid houses with low-interest government loans. Many who otherwise would not have had the funds, attended college on money from the G.I. Bill. Americans who had just survived the Great Depression and a World War looked forward to a period of peace.

But overseas, the war had not really ended. After Japan's surrender, the Chinese Communist party led by Mao Zedong took over all of China but the island of Formosa (now Taiwan) by 1949. That same year, Joseph Stalin ordered a test of the first Soviet atomic bomb. The bomb exploded successfully, soaking a remote corner of Kazakhstan in radiation. Stalin now felt confident enough to go on the offensive against American-held territory in Asia.

Stalin was never happy with the division of Berlin into Eastern and Western sectors; the city was in Soviet territory as he saw it, and therefore should be fully controlled by the Soviets. In 1948, he blockaded West Berlin. The United States military airlifted supplies over the blockade and kept the West Berliners well-fed. This shocked and dismayed Stalin so much that he called off the blockade and turned his focus to the other country that had been divided after The Second World War: Korea.

The Thirty-Eighth Parallel divided the peninsula into  North Korea and South Korea. The North, led by a Communist dictator named Kim Il Sung, had the support of Russia and China while the U.S. backed South Korea. In 1950, Stalin gave Kim Il Sung permission to invade the south. The U.S. military, in support of South Korea, intervened.

Soon after the conflict began, Stalin removed Russian support, leaving Kim Il Sun reliant upon China for military support. For the second time in less than a decade, the United States was at war. The Korean War is often called "The Forgotten War" because many Americans seem disinterested in the conflict our its outcomes. Unlike WWII, the Korean War did not begin with a large-scale attack on the United States.

Also, industry did not mobilize Americans on the home-front at the same scale, and Americans never had to sacrifice gas or food through rationing for the Korean War in the way they had during WWII. Many American homes, instead, reached unprecedented levels of prosperity. Korea seemed like a distant war fought for unclear reasons. It ended in 1953 with a ceasefire, not a peace treaty, and a war with unclear goals also had an ambiguous ending.

Not long after the Korean conflict ended, the United States exploded a new hydrogen bomb at Bikini Atoll as part of the Castle Bravo thermonuclear test program. A hydrogen bomb essentially creates a solar flare that is ten miles in diameter, as hot as the sun, and releases highly radioactive materials over long distances. The first successful detonation of a hydrogen bomb, called Ivy Mike, took place in 1952.

A year after that, in 1953, a young actor from rural Indiana, named James Dean, made his debut in a big-film starring role when he played Cal Trask in *East of Eden*. The movie, based on a John Steinbeck novel about generations of a family in Salinas, California, was the perfect debut role for the brooding Dean. Dean's good looks and tortured-soul persona attracted the attention of movie-goers and the affections of many female fans.

Dean was in his early 20's, just four years older than Elvis, but looked younger. For the last several years, Hollywood's hottest actor had been Marlon Brando, but by 1954 Brando was entering his thirties, and America's new generation of teenage movie patrons were looking for someone closer to their age and generation to idolize. Dean came along at the perfect time.

After he made East of Eden, the studio executives at Warner Bros. cast James Dean in a B-movie titled *Rebel Without a Cause* that was slated to be released in less-expensive black-and-white footage. The technology to make color pictures was available, but costly, and therefore the studio reserved color for bigger-budget

Elvis and Ed Sullivan October 1956 Elvis appeared on The *Ed Sullivan Show* three times from September 9, 1953 to his final appearance on January 6th, 1957.

films that featured Hollywood stars. *Rebel Without a Cause* had originated, not as a screenplay, but as a title. A psychologist had used the title for his academic study of teenage psychopathy. Warner Bros. executives bought the rights to the book title, thinking that they could slap a screenplay behind it and sell a few tickets.

However, while James Dean was filming his second movie, his first one garnered an audience, good reviews, and high-ticket sales. Warner Bros. upgraded *Rebel Without a Cause* to an "A" picture and made it in color. James Dean, only twenty-four-years old, now starred in a major motion picture.

A month before the release of *Rebel Without a Cause,* on September 30, 1955, James Dean and his German mechanic got into Dean's newly purchased limited-edition Porsche 550. Built for speed, not safety (it resembled a soapbox derby car with a small jet engine), the sports car needed to be handled carefully. While Dean unquestionably drove fast, it's not clear if he was speeding or otherwise driving unsafely when a Ford sedan crashed into him. Probably, the sun blinded the driver of the sedan so that he couldn't see the little Porsche. James Dean died at the scene of the accident.

A month later, when teenagers flocked to see *Rebel Without a Cause*, they watched the ghost of James Dean play a troubled sixteen-year-old named Jim Stark. The big Hollywood studios used to have to market their movies as being good for public morals, and anything with lurid themes or splashy violence had to be depicted as a cautionary tale about anti-social behavior. *Rebel Without a Cause* was supposed to scare teens straight.

Audiences, however, tended to overlook the movie's message. The film glorifies violence. Three teenagers are depicted as being killed in the film; two are killed by gunfire. In the course of a day, Jim Stark gets into a knife fight in the parking lot of a Hollywood observatory, drives a stolen car up to the edge of a cliff in a "chicky run," physically attacks his own father, and pulls back his arm at one point as if to punch his own mother. His love interest in the movie, Judy, played by Natalie Wood is a good-girl-gone-bad, who fixates on the "new kid" Jim Stark as an outlet for her own revolutionary impulses.

A homosexual subplot featuring another teenager named Plato, played by Sal Mineo, might had slipped by most of the audience at the time. But there are scenes where Plato clearly seems romantically inclined toward Jim Stark, and even invites Jim to stay the night and have breakfast in the morning. A young Dennis Hopper had a minor but memorable role as a maniacal teen gang member. Although lurid and full of plot holes (Judy sure does get over her dead boyfriend in a hurry), the movie somehow captured the fraught period of mid-adolescence.

Teenage audiences didn't see a cautionary tale; the high-schoolers who ate popcorn in the rows saw how cool James Dean looked with his slicked hair, white t-shirt, and dangling cigarette. Those teenagers left the theater prepared to emulate their silver-screen hero. But James Dean was dead. Like every great performer, he left his audience wanting more. Teenagers felt that a cultural void needed to be filled by a young rebel with cool looks and long hair.

In July of 1954, Sam Phillips released "That's All Right, Mama" to local radio stations. In 1954, radio was a highly interactive medium. If a song came out before there was a record for sale, then the only way listeners could hear the song was if a radio DJ played it over the airwaves. The phones started ringing almost as soon as local DJ's played Elvis' first song and didn't quit for a long time.

Sam Phillips knew he needed to capitalize fast on the song's popularity, but records came out with two sides: an "A" side and a "B" side. He knew what the "A" song would be, but what about the "B" side? In a hurry to get production moving, Elvis and Sam settled on "Blue Moon of Kentucky," a bluegrass/hillbilly tune popularized by the country singer Bill Monroe back in 1946. Elvis and the boys in his band discovered that song, too, by jumping around and having fun.

As soon as the record came out, Elvis went on a local tour, but he and his band only knew a couple of songs, and nobody knew what rock n' roll music was yet. A white singer with a couple of guitar players was expected to play bluegrass or hillbilly music, not dance around onstage singing amped-versions of the Delta Blues. In October of 1954, Elvis played the Grand Ol' Opry.

Playing the Opry was an honor for any southern singer. Elvis got to meet Bill Monroe, the original singer of "Blue Moon of

Kentucky." Monroe was less-than-flattered by Elvis' version of the hillbilly hit, and supposedly had threatened to punch Elvis in the nose. The punch never came, Monroe was genteel when he met Elvis. The audience at the Opry didn't seem to know how to react to this young man in front of them, playing music that was not quite hillbilly and not quite the blues.

Elvis needed to find a new crowd.

The first press writer to interview Elvis could only focus on Elvis' acne, his greasy hair, and his monosyllabic responses to questions. The article indicated that this young man from Tupelo was not yet ready to be a star. Still, DJ's kept playing Elvis' songs and the demand to see him perform live started to grow. Elvis played the Louisiana Hayride once before, back in August of 1955, but this was to be his first headline performance.

Elvis, called The Hillbilly Cat, hit the stage with a new sense of presence. Starting with "That's All Right, Mama" he went on to play "Baby, Let's Play House" (his first original hit), and then a cover of Chuck Berry's hit "Maybelline." Elvis, just twenty years old, bounced around the stage with youthful vigor. Elvis' stage presence riled the young ladies, and a few older ones too, into such an orgiastic fit of screaming and dancing that they nearly mobbed the stage. Frank Sinatra could make the ladies sigh and melt, but Elvis had a different effect from anything ever seen before.

In January of 1955, just after he turned twenty, Elvis hired a new drummer. His name was DJ Fontana, and he'd perfected his technique playing the drums in a Louisiana strip club. When the ladies on the club's stage wiggled, Fontana banged his drums in rhythm with the ensuing jiggles. Now, Fontana could play the same trick with Elvis' onstage shakes.

In November of that year, Elvis watched *Rebel Without a Cause*. He came out of the theater with a new persona.

## Chapter Four

# The Colonel

In May of 1929, in the town of Breda, Holland, the body of Anna van den Enden, the 23-year-old new wife of a grocer, was discovered just behind her husband's grocery store. The young woman died of a blunt force trauma so severe that it knocked part of her brain out of the skull. Whoever killed her also likely tore through the living area attached to the store, and then scattered paper around Enden's body to hide his scent from any police dogs.

The police never found the murderer, but the discovery of the crime coincided exactly with the disappearance of a twenty-year old man named Andre van Kuijk, who lived just a few blocks away from where Enden's body was found. Andre was a knockabout from the Rotterdam area. Just four years before, when Andre was only sixteen, his father had died and Andre had to go find work wherever possible to help support his mother and siblings. A strong lad, he tended to find jobs as a day-laborer.

Planning to go to the United States, Andre took work as a deckhand on a ship. On the day after Anna van dan Enden's death, Andre skipped work. He apparently then visited his sister and acted strangely, shaking the hand of his new-born nephew as if to say farewell. After that, Andre failed to show up to work for two months, at which point his employer sent a trunk with Andre's belongings to his family. It appeared that when Andre disappeared, he had done so in a rush. He didn't even bother to get the money he'd saved from the trunk. His family had no idea where he had gone.

A little while after his disappearance, Andre's siblings received a letter saying that Andre had left. The signature on the letter had two names: Andre and Tom Parker.

It appears that Andre entered the United States illegally at some point in 1929 and found work as a carnival barker. At that time, Americans didn't have social security numbers and most states didn't require driver's licenses (in rural areas, cars remained unusual sights). It was easy for a man to change names, adopt a false past, and start life over as a new person. Traveling carnivals, common in the 1920's, often featured sleazy entertainments and rigged games. Andre started to learn the great American trade of separating customers from their dollars. Still, carnival income is unsteady so Andre looked for something more stable. He joined the Army and adopted the name of the military recruiter, Tom Parker, who conducted the interview. Then Andre, now Tom Parker, sent his letter home.

The army stationed Parker on a base in Hawaii and at some point in 1931, he went Absent Without Leave, possibly to join a circus where he may have worked with elephants. Eventually, he returned to the army base. Parker's superior officers prosecuted him for desertion, and he went into solitary confinement for several months. The punishment caused a psychotic break so severe that the Army had to discharge Parker and he moved back to the contiguous United States.

After his stint in the army, Parker mostly earned a living working various jobs in the carnival trade. Despite what seems to have been a lifelong disinterest in women, he got married to Marrie Francis Mott in 1935 right in the heart of The Great Depression. In 1938, Parker turned the talents he had developed as a carnival barker to the music promotional trade. He began by selling tickets for faded hillbilly-music stars but eventually signed a contract for a percentage of the earnings made by Eddy Arnold, who was a popular attraction at the time.

In the 1930's and 1940's musical acts toured from small town to small town just like the carnival, so Parker was familiar with the lifestyle. He had a gift for gaudy promotions that gelled well with the country acts of the era. Audiences in little towns expected to see some glitz and glamour from the musical acts, so performers came out on stage glittering with rhinestones. Female singers often styled their hair into tall mounds and wore large swooping dresses. Elvis would eventually learn many of his showman's techniques from this environment, and Tom Parker knew the tricks better than anyone. At some point, and for reasons that are unclear, Tom

Parker added the honorific of "Colonel" to his name. He went by "Colonel Tom Parker" or just "The Colonel" for the rest of his life. In 1953, Eddy Arnold parted ways with Tom Parker. Col. Parker focused on promoting his new act, the Canadian country-singer Hank Snow. Managing Snow was Parker's primary job when Parker first heard Elvis Presley in 1955. Like a lot of people, Parker's first encounter with Elvis was when he heard "That's All Right, Mama" over the radio. Parker thought Elvis had to be a black vocalist, something which would have closed a lot of promotional avenues in the mid-1950's. When he found out that Elvis was white, Parker became intrigued.

Elvis already had a manager, a Memphis DJ named Bob Neal, who had the trust of Elvis' parents. However, Neal didn't have the industry contacts or promotional expertise that Parker did. Parker worked his way closer to Elvis, and eventually had a meeting with both Neal and the singer. They cut a deal to let Parker be co-manager, but from that point on in 1955, Colonel Tom Parker managed Elvis Presley.

The first and most obvious step for Parker was to have Elvis break up with Sam Phillips and Sun Records. Sun Records did not have a national distribution network, and if Elvis was to reach his full potential (and full earning potential) as an act, then he would have to sign with a record label capable of making Elvis' music available nationwide, like the Radio Corporation of America (RCA),

On November 21, 1955, just three weeks after the nationwide release of *Rebel Without a Cause*, and not quite two months after the death of James Dean, Elvis signed a contract with RCA records. A famous photograph from the time period shows, Col. Tom Parker with his hand on Gladys Presley's shoulder while she planted a smooch on her son's cheek. Elvis' dad, Vernon, looked on appreciatively. Elvis, flanked by his parents and immersed in a success he never could have dreamed of just a few years earlier, wore a grin.

Parker, a carnie salesman to his core, knew he had the ultimate attraction in Elvis. Fans paid money to listen to the singer's voice, and they bought tickets to see Elvis shimmy, shake, and emote through his songs. Almost none of the teenage girls who shouted themselves into ecstasy from the crowds knew anything about or cared to know anything about the boys in the band. Parker, who was keeping a hefty, even unheard-of-for-the-industry, twenty-five percent of Elvis' profits put the band members on a salary. If they didn't like it, the Colonel figured, there were plenty of other guitar and drum players in Memphis.

At some point, early in 1956, just as Elvis' fame started to peak, the young singer caught the attention of Natalie Wood. Wood was just eighteen but had been a movie star for half her life. In 1947, at age nine, Wood had starred in the perennial holiday classic Miracle on Thirty-Fourth Street as a girl who had grown up too fast and expressed some skepticism about the reality of Santa Claus. Elvis was just three years older than Wood, but he had seen her in Miracle and then again in Rebel. Intrigued by Elvis, Wood asked her Rebel co-star, Dennis Hopper, to introduce them.

Not long after they first met, Natalie gifted Elvis a velvet shirt. When he performed a homecoming concern in Tupelo, Mississippi, Elvis donned the gift and expressed to friends that life seemed just about perfect. However, when he invited Natalie Wood to meet his parents, the brief romance quickly dissolved. Natalie felt that Elvis, when not on stage, could be sort of dull. Also, Glady clearly intended to be the main woman in Elvis' life. Gladys disapproved of Wood's sometimes-revealing fashion choices, her Hollywood-starlet demeanor, and her seemingly physical interest in Elvis. When twenty-one-year-old Elvis sat on his mother's lap, this was too much for Wood, who made up an excuse to leave and never came back.

Just as Elvis' early period of fame seemed to be peaking, a backlash to the new teen youth culture brewed in some of the socially conservative circles. Some of this came from an inevitable clash between the 1950's youth culture and Americans over twenty-five. In the 1950's, adulthood came quickly; marriages occurred in the teen years and a high percentage of seventeen- and eighteen-year-old young women wore engagement rings to their high school graduations.

In the 1950's, teenagers shared cultural space in the United States with previous generations who lived through the First World War, the Great Depression, the Second World War, and then the Korean War. For black Americans, segregation and racial oppression made

Elvis on his 1956 Pepper Red Harley-Davidson KH that was powered by a 883cc Flathead engine.

all of these trials worse. Suddenly, teenagers had time to languish for eighteen years in school. They played sports, wore letterman jackets, and listened to new records on the juke box at the local drug store and soda fountain. Elvis seemed a flippant form of entertainment to many war veterans. This new culture fixated on youth seemed unserious at a time when the Soviet Union seemed to be such a threat.

*Rebel Without a Cause* was not the only film about wayward teenagers to cause a stir in 1955. That was also the year that *The Blackboard Jungle*, about an English teacher trying to educate teens in a segregated school, debuted on screens. Like *Rebel*, the movie included lurid depictions of wayward youth, but unlike *Rebel*, the main character was an adult authority figure with short hair and a suit. *The Blackboard Jungle* also featured a new Hollywood gimmick; it included a soundtrack with popular music. About the time that Elvis cut "That's Alright, Mama" Bill Haley and his Comets released the iconic "Rock Around the Clock." It was featured in The Blackboard Jungle, forever connecting the emerging rock n' roll sound with the fears and excitement inherent with teenager rebellion.

Col. Tom Parker and Hollywood movie producers started to recognize just how much money could be made promoting Elvis, teenage rebellion, and rock n' roll music -- the very things preachers were condemning. Bill Haley made good music and young women would dance to his songs, but he couldn't send them into a craze like Elvis. Elvis Presley became the face of rock n' roll and his swinging hips were about to cause a revolution.

Those hips were about to shake on a new medium that was also taking over the country: television.

## Chapter Five

# Ed Sullivan

After WWII, just a few wealthy households could afford television sets. Televisions (TV's) were large, like any other piece of furniture, and had knobs up by a rounded screen for turning the channel. Television stations broadcast programs via antennas and most TV's only picked up two or three channels. In the late 1940's, when most Americans still listened to news and entertainment on the radio, there weren't many programs available to be watched on a TV anyway. That started to change in 1948, with the debut of *The Ed Sullivan Show* which aired over Central Broadcasting Systems (CBS).

Radio had been ideal for variety programs, where different types of music, comedy, or interviews could be featured on the same show. That was the thinking behind *The Ed Sullivan Show* as well; viewers could be treated to several different kinds of acts. Sullivan himself may have become TV's first household name. Between 1948 and 1955, the price of televisions shrank considerably as average incomes rose; more homes tuned in for the CBS's primetime broadcast. By 1955, a large television featured in the living rooms of more than half of American homes.

In this, the United States lagged behind only England. In the spring of 1953, Englanders had gone on a mad spending spree to buy "the box" so they could watch the coronation of young Queen Elizabeth II. It seemed surreal to the average Brit that something as fanciful as the coronation of a queen could be broadcast into millions of living rooms. More than half the country watched Elizabeth II become queen and the place of television in English life was set.

Sullivan, who had once been a multi-sport athlete in his home state of New York, walked with an odd square-shouldered posture, as if his neck didn't rotate. He started almost every program by saying "Tonight, we have a really big show," only it sounded like he said. "Tonight, we have a really big shew." People loved to imitate him, and Sullivan had a charismatic ability to laugh at himself. If Elizabeth II was coronated as queen in Westminster Abbey by the Archbishop of Canterbury, then Ed Sullivan would do the same for rock n' roll by making Elvis the King.

However, at first Sullivan didn't understand the appeal of Elvis and showed little interest in booking him. In 1955, Elvis made a few appearances of less-watched programs, like the *Milton Berle Show*, but Sullivan didn't bring him on. Part of this had to do with Elvis' growing sex appeal; girls just couldn't control themselves around him.

In 1955, Elvis played a series of shows in Jacksonville, Florida. A group of female fans jumped up on stage and nearly tore his clothes off. Sometimes, Elvis would start singing then find himself standing ankle-deep in the lacy underpants thrown on-stage by his most ardent fans. A red-blooded American boy, Elvis certainly sowed his oats with many a groupie before and after his shows. He didn't need to charm women, they sometimes hid in his hotel rooms and popped out from underneath the bed when he entered.

Elvis' unwholesome effect on women, plus his growing fame, inspired many a sermon against him. One Jacksonville preacher, Revered Robert Gray, held an open Bible at a prayer service while he condemned Elvis. Gray insinuated that Elvis Presley would almost certainly refuse the gift of Jesus's salvation if it was offered to him. Elvis and his parents found this kind of attack, and there were many, perplexing. Elvis was raised a Pentecostal, often prayed before his shows, and still attended services with his mother and father when time allowed.

Elvis had always loved the blues, hillbilly music, and gospel in equal parts and saw nothing anti-religious in his lyrics. He couldn't help it if the ladies went wild when he shook his hips; he'd been dancing like that since he was ten years old. A twenty-something Elvis couldn't resist laying with all those young women who flocked around him, but in southern Christian circles, a young man sinning out of lust was a relatively minor offense.

In late January of 1956, RCA began the nationwide release of Elvis' music with a two-sided record. The "A" side featured

"Heartbreak Hotel," with Elvis at his emotive best. No one else could have sung the tune and made it a hit; the song had a slow and seductive rhythm coupled with clumsy lyrics, but it was perfect for Elvis' primary audience of young women.

A morbid legend, maybe apocryphal, soon connected itself to the song. The song's authors were Mae Baren Axton and Tommy Durden. The former was a high school teacher and the latter a well-known songwriter. They claimed that the idea for the song's first stanza "Ever since my baby she left me, I found a new place to dwell; it's down at the end of lonely street at heartbreak hotel" had its origins in a suicide note. They claimed to have read a story in a Miami newspaper about a man who left the phrase "I walk a lonely street" in a note he left behind just before committing suicide. No one was ever able to find that particular story in any newspaper, however, so the song's authors could have just been playing with the media.

When he first heard the song, Elvis loved it and quickly memorized the lyrics. A pause between beats early in the song gave Elvis the chance to thrust his hips out, and then he could coo into the microphone to his adoring fans on the next beat. It

Elvis signing autographs in 1956 during an appearance in Minneapolis, MN.

was a song perfect for an Elvis performance, and for an audience of emotionally charged teenagers. However, few people outside of that demographic liked the song. Sam Phillips spoke for many when he called "Heartbreak Hotel" a "morbid mess." The "B" side featured "I got a Woman" which is technically a superior song, but not one Elvis could perform with so much emotional power.

One day after the release of his first RCA record, Elvis appeared on the Central Broadcasting Station (CBS) program called *Stage Show*. RCA's plan had been for Elvis to play "Heartbreak Hotel," but the song seemed so disjointed that the *Stage Show*'s producers feared that audiences would hate it. Elvis seemed to be the only one who had confidence in the song. He was scheduled for three performances on the program, and finally, on his last one on February 4, he convinced the show's producers to let him sing his new favorite tune.

Audiences went wild over the performance, and less than ten weeks later, "Heartbreak Hotel" stood atop both the popular charts and the country-and-western music charts. By the spring of 1956, the "Heartbreak Hotel" record had sold a million copies. It seemed natural that America's biggest musical act should stage an appearance on America's most popular television show.

Ed Sullivan continued to resist as he was still unsure what to make of Elvis. For millions of American teenagers, an Elvis appearance on Ed Sullivan would mean making their favorite singer more acceptable to adults. If Elvis appeared on a family-friendly program, like Ed Sullivan, then he couldn't be as dangerous as all those preachers were making him out to be. In this, Ed Sullivan stood as an archetype for many of America's disapproving fathers. If Sullivan would accept Elvis, then millions of parents would too.

Meanwhile, Elvis kept recording music. His next RCA hit was more bizarre than his first one. He performed a song that a black female artist, Big Mama Thornton, had sold half-a-million copies singing in 1953. The song "Hound Dog" is a blues song clearly meant to be sung by a woman. A "hound dog" who was "cryin' all the time" was understood by most listeners to be a sexually excited man whining to his woman in hopes of receiving some physical love.

Yet, audiences who loved Elvis' voice and on-stage presence

didn't seem to care much about the lyrics, and "Hound Dog" was a catchy rhythm and blues song that had a beat designed to get people up and dancing. In April of 1956, Elvis performed "Hound Dog" live on the flight deck of a U.S. naval aircraft carrier in San Diego, California. Col. Tom Parker had pulled that one off somehow and seemed to love being deferred to by real naval officers. By that time, Parker insinuated he was from West Virginia and didn't seem to mind if enlisted men assumed him to be a real Colonel.

"Hound Dog's" rhythm gave full release to Elvis' hips, something that drove all the ladies into hysterics. The authorities continued to condemn Elvis, and so did Ed Sullivan. There were no plans to have Elvis shake around on *The Ed Sullivan Show*. That may have been the end of the discussion except for the fact that the National Broadcasting Corporation (NBC) had decided to challenge *The Ed Sullivan Show*'s lock on primetime ratings. NBC's executives decided to run the *Steve Allen Show* (starring comedian and radio personality, Steve Allen as host) in the same time slot as Ed Sullivan. Allen had few compunctions about inviting Elvis onto his program, and on July 1, 1956, Elvis made his primetime television debut. He would sing "Hound Dog" live ... to a hound dog.

Steve Allen wanted the ratings boom that Elvis could bring, but

This photo was sent out by the CBS television program Stage Show (hosted by the Dorsey Brothers Jimmy & Tommy) to promote the first national television appearance of Elvis on January 28, 1956.

A photo of Elvis performing with Scotty Moore (center) and Bill Black (right) appeared in TV Radio Mirror for their September 1956 issue.

he also worried that a negative reaction to an Elvis performance could bring a quick end to his show. Allen decided to try and make a comedy-bit out of Elvis' appearance. To introduce the act, Allen stood awkwardly before his live audience and stated he was committed to making sure that his show was something the whole family could enjoy and then, tellingly, said "this is the new Elvis" when he introduced his guest.

Elvis walked on stage, black hair slicked back, wearing a tuxedo. At that point, Allen pointed to a Bassett Hound in a top hat who was sitting laconically on a table. The audience soon realized that Elvis would be singing to this hound. The bit got some nervous laughs from the live audience, but most of Elvis' teenaged fans found the performance perplexing. What did Allen mean by the "new Elvis?" Why was Elvis in a tux, and where were his fast-moving hips? Elvis hated the act and found the whole thing a very public humiliation. Nonetheless, the *Steve Allen Show* received higher ratings that night than Sullivan faced irrelevance if he did not bring Elvis on.

Just a few months before, Col. Parker was willing to accept

$5,000 as payment for an appearance on the *Ed Sullivan Show*, but now that Ed was doing the asking, Parker would not take less than $50,000. This meant that Elvis would be making, for three performances totaling about fifteen minutes, half as much as President Eisenhower made for the whole year. Elvis was set to play on *Ed Sullivan's Sunday Night Showcase*, on September 9th, 1956.

Col. Tom Parker believed that Elvis' good looks and charm would be perfect for the silver screen. He managed to have Elvis cast in a musical-western picture, called *The Reno Brothers*. Elvis did not star in the movie but would play guitar and sing a new song called "Don't Be Cruel." Parker had negotiated an impressive entertainment trifecta: Elvis would play a new song in a movie, and then promote both the movie and the song on the nation's most-watched prime-time television program.

Unfortunately, in early August, Sullivan received serious injuries in a head-on car collision while driving to his home in Connecticut. He lay in a hotel bed, recovering from the wreck, when Elvis made his first appearance. A famous British thespian named Charles Loughton filled in for Ed Sullivan, and he was the one who introduced Elvis Presley.

Presley, dressed in a checked shirt and matching blazer, brought

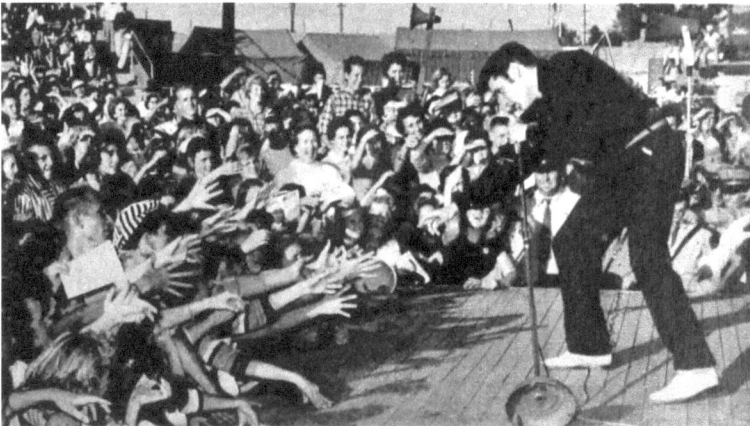

Elvis performs live for TV Radio Mirror at the Mississippi-Alabama Fairgrounds in September of 1957.

the full Elvis experience to the performance. His black hair was greased to perfection, and his smile made millions of viewers feel as if he was right there in the living room with them. Elvis started off with a new song, "Don't Be Cruel" that was a perfect showcase for his talents. Elvis still wiggled around on stage, but the slower tempo of "Don't Be Cruel" kept Elvis from dancing too suggestively in front of any prudish viewers.

No Bassett hound was present to provide comic relief, but Elvis' backup singers, dressed in bowties, lightened the atmosphere. Elvis followed up with the ballad "Love Me Tender" and made a heartfelt get-well wish to Ed Sullivan. High Schoolers everywhere showed up at school that next day talking about the performance and for many it defined their teenage years.

"Don't be Cruel" sold so well that it not only hit number one on the charts, but it convinced the producers of *The Reno Brothers* musical western to change the name of the movie to *Don't Be Cruel*. The release of the first Elvis movie came on November 15, 1956, right in the middle of Elvis' three *Ed Sullivan Show* performances.

The first Ed Sullivan appearance featured Elvis Presley at his "aw-shucks" best. The songs maximized his vocal talents while minimizing his hip movement. He mesmerized a massive American audience while at the same time placating some of his critics. Maybe most importantly, Elvis' good-natured personality endeared him to Ed Sullivan and his staff.

Elvis made two more appearances on *The Ed Sullivan Show*, the last of which took place on January 6, 1957, one day after Presley's 22nd birthday. Sullivan had recovered enough by that time to return and he said this, on air, to Presley: "I wanted to say to Elvis Presley and the country that this is a real decent, fine boy, and wherever you go, Elvis, we want to say we've never had a pleasanter experience on our show with a big name than we've had with you."

It amounted to an endorsement of Elvis, his music, and youth culture. But there were new names coming into the rock n' roll scene, and the Soviet space program was just a few months away from sending a man-made satellite into orbit, and Americans into a panic.

## Chapter Six

# All Shook Up

Elvis needed a break from being famous, but he seemed caught up in something he couldn't control. Even before *The Ed Sullivan Show* appearances there were signs that he could no longer expect any kind of normal life. In October of 1956, Elvis eased his long white Cadillac Continental into a Memphis gas station. Fans recognized the luxury car as belonging to Elvis and swarmed around it for autographs. Drivers who just wanted a tank of gas couldn't get to the pumps and the frustrated station owner, Ed Hopper, shouted for Elvis to move the Cadillac out of the way.

Elvis tried to comply, but when he didn't move fast enough, Hopper put his arm through the driver window and smacked Elvis on the back of the head. Elvis jumped out of the Cadillac and popped Hopper in the eye with a right cross. Both Elvis and Hopper got hauled into court for the altercation, and Hopper was found to be guilty and issued a fine. It was a minor incident, but Elvis had never been in any real trouble in his life and disliked being put into a position where he couldn't be liked.

And the women. Women everywhere. All the time. Elvis loved them. Young women he just met would flirt with him, and often Elvis would touch tongues with women who just fell into his embrace. Girls would hold Elvis' hand and snuggle up to him as if they had known him forever. Elvis was romantic by nature, loved women, and could seduce just about any pretty young thing he met with just a smile and his presence. Some of the young men in his entourage could not believe the scale of Elvis' sexual appetite.

After the Ed Sullivan appearances, Elvis reached a level of fame that no other entertainer had ever attained. He also entered his most creative phase as a musical artist, and arguably his two best songs, "All Shook Up" and "Jailhouse Rock" were released in the spring and early fall of 1957 just before the Soviets sent Sputnik into the stratosphere.

"All Shook Up" debuted on April 13, 1957, and shimmied to the top of the Billboard pop chart right away. It was a fun rock n' roll song, with Elvis singing "I'm itchin' like a man on a fuzzy tree" and pining for a mythical woman whose "...lips are like a volcano that's hot." It was Elvis at his flirty best, singing a song that seemed both harmless and sexy at the same time.

Elvis paid little attention to finances and Col. Tom Parker took advantage. As long as Elvis kept enough money on hand to buy what he wanted and to dole out generous gifts to friends, he seemed unconcerned about how much his manager kept. In March of 1957, Elvis purchased his Graceland mansion and estate in Memphis in what may have been the most ostentatious purchase a twenty-two-year-old had ever made. And Parker had a brilliant plan to maximize revenues.

Parker knew nothing about the movie business, but he knew that people would pay money to see Elvis play music on the big screen. Well before *Music Television* (MTV) debuted music videos in the 1980's, Parker conceived of a movie that had performances set to new music. In September of 1957, RCA released the number one hit "Jailhouse Rock." The intent was to give the song time to gain popularity, and then debut a movie with the same name starring Elvis.

In the movie, Elvis played a tough-guy construction worker named Vince Everett. Vince accidentally killed a belligerent drunk in a barroom fist fight and ended up in the state prison. Vince's cell-mate happened to be a down-on-his-luck country singer and guitar player who was willing to impart his musical knowledge to Vince.

Then, as luck would have it, the prisoners had the opportunity to play in a nationally televised amateur prison performance. Vince, with his fellow prisoners, performed a catchy song and dance sequence on camera and this set him up to be a star upon his release. Although the plot was improbable at best, the "Jailhouse Rock" sequence would eventually go down in history as the first musical video. Audiences showed up to marvel at Elvis' face and shimmy with his dance moves. Most probably cared little about the quality of the screenplay. The movie never became the major hit that Col. Tom Parker had hoped it would become, but it grossed a respectable profit.

September and October of 1957 marked the height of Elvis' career, and maybe of his life. His mother and father lived with him in his new mansion, and he strummed and sang some of his career-best music. However, new performers started to appear on the rock n' roll scene, and something new had just appeared in the October sky.

While Elvis made his first movie and appeared on *The Ed Sullivan Show*, another kind of rock n' roll performer brought his sound out of the deep south. Jerry Lee Lewis was just a few months younger than Elvis, and had grown up in the same kind of Depression-era poverty. As a boy, Lewis had worked on the family

Jailhouse Rock premiered in Memphis on Oct 17 and released nationwide on Nov 8, 1957.

farm in Louisiana, and, also like Elvis, had a savant-like ability to sing and play music of all kinds.

While Elvis first performed in public at age ten, Jerry Lee Lewis started at age fourteen when he played hillbilly songs at a car dealership. Jerry Lee's mother worried about her son's sinful ways of playing the piano, and sent him off to a strict Christian school in Texas in hopes that he might use his musical talents to praise God. Lewis did play Christian music but did it so lewdly at a school talent show that he got himself kicked out.

From there, Jerry Lee Lewis wandered up to Mississippi where he started to hear some of the new rock n' roll sounds, and then back to Louisiana where he tried to cut some music in New Orleans, and eventually played for the Louisiana Hayride. By 1955, he was living in Nashville and trying unsuccessfully to sing on the Grand Ol' Opry.

In 1956 Lewis showed up at Sun Records in Memphis, Tennessee, ready to show off his unique musical talents. Phillips recognized Lewis's potential as a money-maker, and Lewis recorded a single called "Crazy Arms" that sold well-enough to

Jailhouse Rock lobby card used inside theaters. It reads "Slugging Elvis Presley went to jail for manslaughter; he didn't mean to kill this tough!"

Elvis' played Vince Everett with his love interest Peggy Van Alden played by Judy Tyler who tragically died in a car accident before the movie premiered.

earn Jerry Lee a following of fans. In 1957, just as conservative America started accepting Elvis Presley, Sam Phillips released "Whole Lotta Shakin' Goin' On" by Jerry Lee Lewis. The song's sexual overtones could hardly be hidden with lyrics like "You can shake one time for me," and "All you gotta do honey is kinda stand in one spot, wiggle around just a little bit."

Rock n' Roll fans who felt let down by Elvis Presley's sudden acceptance by the establishment, could now shimmy and shake to the wild piano playing of Jerry Lee Lewis. At the same time, Col. Parker kept looking to Hollywood for Elvis' future. In *Love Me Tender* Elvis had proved he could act a little bit, and audiences showed they would turn out to see Elvis play music on the big screen. It seemed that Elvis might have a future as a popular entertainer for the whole family.

Then, in October of 1957, the "Chief Designer" of the Soviet space program, a physicist named Sergei Korolev (although at the time no one knew this as his name was classified) had a man-made satellite towed into outer space with a rocket. The satellite, made of aluminum and small enough to fit in the bed of a pickup truck, was called Sputnik which meant "fellow traveler" in Russian.

At the time Korolev faced off in an epic duel of the minds against Werner von Braun, a Nazi rocket scientist who had been captured in 1945 and brought back to the United States as both a VIP and a POW. Braun was the definition of an evil genius. He had used Jewish slave labor to help build his V-2 rocket, the first rockets of any consequence, and the U.S. military repatriated Braun and a slew of other German scientists through a special project known as Operation Paperclip.

In 1957, the U.S. and Soviet militaries occupied themselves, primarily, with trying to create long range rockets capable of

Elvis and co-star Debra Paget posing for *Love Me Tender* Press Photos. The two were romantically involved for a time but eventually parted.

holding thermonuclear warheads. Eventually, both sides would create Intercontinental Ballistic Missiles (ICBM's). Both President Eisenhower, and the Soviet Premier Nikita Khrushchev believe that space exploration should occur as a side effect of the military's prime mission of developing an arsenal of nuclear rockets. Sergei Korolev pursued the creation of his red satellite out of a personal interest in space exploration and the physics of elliptical orbits. Sputnik cost very little to make, and since it was towed into space with a rocket, the biggest part of the expense could be chalked up to military experimentation.

Khrushchev paid almost no attention to the satellite, and the official Soviet newspaper, Pravda (truth), buried the story deep in the October 5th edition the day after the successful launch. When informed of Sputnik, Eisenhower spoke for many in the military when he expressed a lack of concern over an "aluminum beach ball." It was, after all, an era where super-weapons of shocking destructive power seemed to be of foremost concern.

Yet, both Khrushchev and Eisenhower were about to see how the proliferation of television changed everything. The same audiences who tuned in to see Ed Sullivan also watched the nightly news, and Sputnik was a made-for-television moment. Experienced scientists came on the nightly news programs to explain the trajectory of Sputnik's orbit and to marvel over the idea that a Russian-made satellite actually sped around the planet.

At night, ordinary people across the Midwest could look up and see Sputnik moving across the sky, or if they had a special radio, they could listen to the satellite's distinctive beeping sound as it sped across the heavens. Everyone who saw the experts on TV, or who watched the satellite in the sky, or heard it on their radios could recognize one thing: the Soviets, and not the Americans, had done that.

Khrushchev, delighted that a program he knew nothing about made his government look impressive, immediately embraced the idea of Soviet superiority in rocket science and physics. The space race had begun.

Just a few days after Sputnik's launch, even as Americans panicked over a silver ball flying overhead, "Great Balls of Fire" by Jerry Lee Lewis rocked their car stereos and home record players.

The piano had been a feature of "big band" music in the forties, and had been a staple of classical music since the baroque era. But Jerry Lee Lewis did something different to those keys. "Great Balls of Fire" featured the Cajun banging away melodically, while he sang "Goodness gracious, great balls of fire!" into the microphone. Lewis wore his hair long, sang with flash, and generally acted like an arrogant star wherever he played. He possessed none of Elvis' effusive charm, and there was nothing of the mama's boy in Jerry Lee.

Jerry Lee's fame peaked in the fall of 1957, when he was 22 years old. Few people knew it at the time but Jerry Lee, who had already been married twice, had entered into a relationship with his 13-year-old cousin, Myra Gale Brown. The two married in secret, and Jerry remained a star as long as the public remained ignorant of the match.

To millions of young women, Elvis was a heartthrob, and to millions more music fans, Elvis was the King of Rock n' Roll. But to Uncle Sam, Elvis was a healthy young man fit for service. Elvis had become eligible for the draft in January of 1956, just after his twenty-first birthday. Elvis was about to join the army, and many observers thought that Jerry Lee Lewis would be the new King of Rock n' Roll while Elvis was in uniform.

## Chapter Seven

# Drafted

Just two months after "Great Balls of Fire" burned up the radio airwaves, the U.S. Army ordered Elvis Presley to report for duty.

President Truman instituted a peacetime draft in 1948; his concern being that the downsizing of the military post-WWII could leave America vulnerable to Soviet aggression. The draft continued during the Korean War, while Elvis was in high school, but the government kept it in place for peacetime service given the Cold War tensions in Asia and Europe. Given that WWI and WWII had been separated by only two decades, many people felt a Third World War between the United States and the Soviet Union would prove to be inevitable.

Sputnik represented tangible evidence that the Soviet Union possessed the scientific and industrial might to challenge the United States. Older audiences had just begun to accept Elvis, but Elvis, his family, and Col. Tom Parker all realized that if Elvis refused military service or tried to use his fame and wealth in any way to avoid going into the Army, then that acceptance would be rescinded.

Ultimately, Elvis considered himself to be a patriotic American kid. Like most men who got drafted, Elvis looked on the prospect of army life with something less than enthusiasm, but he would go for his two years of service if his country required it. The separation from his mother would be the most troubling thing to him. Elvis adored his mother and had never been separated from her for long. One of the reasons he'd built Graceland was to give her a nice place to live after she'd endured so many hard years of poverty. Gladys seemed not to care much about the mansion, she just wanted to be with her son. For her, the separation would be a devastating event.

Originally, Elvis was scheduled to enter basic training in January of 1958, but Parker had signed a deal with Paramount Pictures to have Elvis make a movie called *King Creole*. If Elvis went into boot camp, then Paramount would be out the $350,000 the company had already invested. Elvis wrote the Draft Board and asked for a delay. His entry date was pushed back to March. Delayed entries were not uncommon in the peacetime draft, but the Draft Board

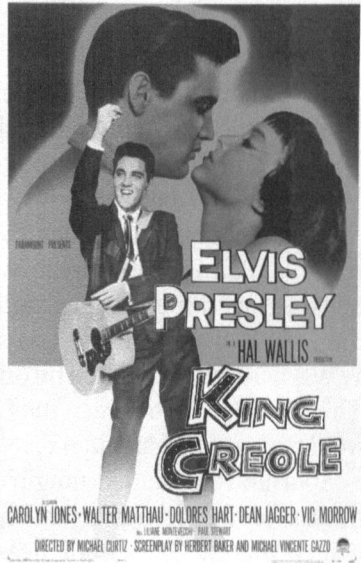

Many fans swarmed New Orleans where Presley and Carolyn Jones were filming. It caused filming delays when the crowds were too large.

received a slew of angry letters about the incident, proving that legions of parents and other authority figures still considered Elvis to be a moral menace to America's youth.

The stress regarding the army situation did not seem to harm Elvis' acting. In *King Creole*, he enjoyed playing a 19-year-old Louisiana boy named Danny Fisher who gets mixed up with some criminal men and a couple of attractive young women. Elvis played "Hard Hearted Woman" for the film's soundtrack. Per Col. Tom Parker's theory, the song-and-movie combination proved profitable as the song went number one on the singles chart and the movie turning into a top-five money maker during its opening week.

Maybe more importantly, Elvis got decent reviews for his acting ability, something that would be important if he was to continue transitioning his career from the musical stage to the big screen. Elvis' solid performance also gave his fans something positive to remember him by as he disappeared from public life for two years.

In March of 1958, just before entering basic training, Elvis Presley threw a party at the Memphis Rainbow Rollerdome. Truth was, he'd been partying for a while, trying to squeeze in several weeks' worth of fun before he entered the basic training dry spell. Elvis was a patriotic American boy, but not so much that he relished leaving Graceland and a life of luxury for the barracks and a life of military toil.

In the past, when celebrities entered the military they tended to be commissioned into Special Services. This had been the case, in 1942, when heavyweight boxing champion Joe Louis had been drafted. Although he went through basic training like everyone else, afterward Louis was mostly expected to make appearances with the troops in order to improve morale. He'd make an appearance, put on light sparring matches, and then shake some hands.

The army offered Elvis a similar opportunity; after basic training he could perform shows for the troops. The offer appalled Col. Tom Parker, however, who could not conceive of the notion that Elvis would play music for free. Even worse, the U.S. Army would then own the rights to any profits from Elvis' shows or other promotions. Additionally, although Elvis was less than enthused about military service, he also showed no interest in being treated as a special case. If he was going in, he wanted to be treated like any other army grunt.

As his induction date got closer, Elvis became more agitated. The term of service for draftees was two years, and Elvis knew how long that could be in the music world. His fans could easily move on to any of the new acts that were quickly coming onto the rock n' roll scene. Col. Parker thought this was not true, believing that Elvis' stint in the army would make him more popular with older Americans, and that the time away would prevent overexposure.

Col. Parker knew a money-making spectacle when he saw one,

Elvis being sworn into the Army March of 1958 (top).
Elvis poses beside a tank while serving in Germany. His
patch reads "SPEARHEAD" (bottom).

and he intended to squeeze every last dime out of Elvis' last few days and hours as a civilian. For three days, the media trailed Elvis. They took pictures of him saying a tearful goodbye to Gladys, of Elvis looking pensive at a diner while he breakfasted with the Colonel himself, and most importantly of a barber shaving off Elvis' famous greasy black hair. In the last picture, Elvis looked almost playful as he blew a nearly shorn lock off his palm.

The reality of army service didn't seem to fully set in until Elvis had to strip down to his white underwear and raise his hands over his head just like all the other recruits. A famous picture caught the moment, and the expression on Elvis' face tells it all. He was in the army now; Elvis Presley now went by Private First Class Presley.

After he checked in at Memphis, the Army sent Elvis to Fort Hood, Texas where he trained with a tank battalion. At first, the other soldiers, assuming he was a pampered celebrity, picked on Elvis a little. Elvis was nothing if not likable, though, and he soon made friends with his fellow G.I.'s. He was always generous with his money and even bought spare uniforms for his barracks mates in

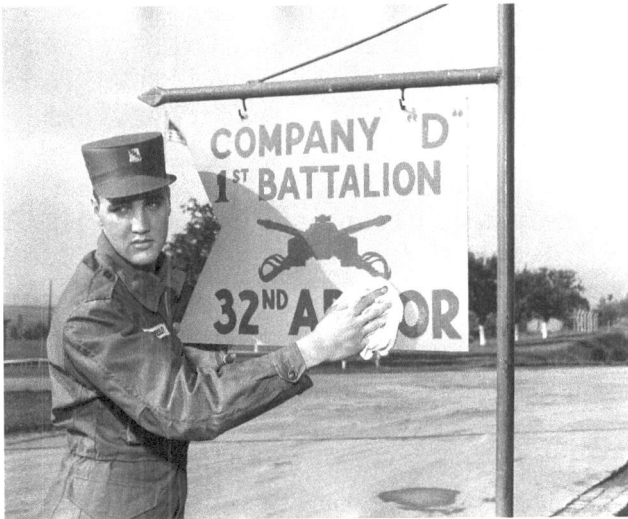

Towards the end of his tour, Elvis qualified at the rank of Sergeant E-5, serving in Company D, 1 – 32 Armor. Elvis' uniform is on display at the Patton Museum of Cavalry and Armor at Ft. Knox, Kentucky,

basic training.

Elvis never asked for, nor did he receive, any special treatment. His willingness to perform the same tasks as everyone else soon meant he became just one of the guys. None of his fellow soldiers ever said a bad word about Elvis to the press; all of them attested to the same thing: Elvis did his duty like everyone else, and was as generous to people in the military as he was to everyone in civilian life. The pay he received for his service went to charity.

Like many draftees who went through basic training, Elvis put on a tough face in front of the other men but revealed his true feelings through his letters and phone calls home. He was still just twenty-three years old, and had never been separated from his mother for so long. When he did get to make the occasional phone call to his mother, both he and Gladys would cry for most of an hour.

Basic training finally ended in June, and Elvis emerged as a sharpshooter with the Army tank division. Like everybody else, he got a short break after basic training and used the opportunity to record a few songs before reporting back to Fort Hood. This time, he could live away from the army base with his family. The reunion with his loved ones immediately cheered Elvis.

Col. Tom Parker, in the meanwhile, had pivoted his money-making schemes. If Elvis could not perform live, or make movies while in the army, then Parker would have to make money on Elvis merchandise. Stores across the country stocked lunch boxes, t-shirts, coffee mugs, and buttons with the likeness of Elvis Presley on them. Parker kept a hefty percentage of the merchandise profits, and it was hard for Elvis to maintain his image as a rebel given that his face now adorned lunchboxes, but the merchandise did define Elvis' image for a younger generation.

Glady Presley had always suffered from a nervous constitution, and she tended to medicate her anxiety with junk food and alcohol. With Elvis away in basic training, Gladys increased her consumption of both and spent her days worrying. She put on weight and then tried to take it off with diet pills. The combination of stress, poor eating habits, and consumption of pills and booze caused her health to decline rapidly. Although only forty-six, she became seriously ill in early August of 1958 while living in Texas with Elvis and Vernon.

As her health deteriorated, so did her relationship with her husband. One day, after an argument with Vernon, she fell so seriously ill that she had to be hospitalized a day later. Elvis tried to get an emergency medical leave to be with his mother, but his sergeant denied the request and Elvis threatened to desert so that he could be with his mom. On August 12, the Army finally granted an emergency family leave. Elvis rushed to his mother's side. Gladys died two days later from a combination of cirrhosis of the liver, which was either caused or exacerbated by her heavy drinking, and from a heart attack.

The funeral took place in the heat of mid-August and Elvis fell down from grief several times during the service. His mother had been the most precious thing in his life, and Elvis could not come to terms with her death. The Army allows just a little time for soldiers to grieve and just a few days after the funeral, Elvis found out he would be stationed in West Germany.

Elvis was sent to Brooklyn, New York where he engaged in a short press conference before shipping out on September 22. When Elvis got to Germany, the army assigned him to chauffeur the commanding officer. The army officer, put off by seeing enlisted men so excited to see his driver, reassigned Elvis to drive someone less senior.

Before he'd gotten drafted, Elvis had recorded dozens of songs with RCA. RCA's executives planned to slowly release Elvis' songs until their star could return from service. This meant that while he was living in West Germany, Elvis could claim to have over forty songs make the top ten. "A Big Hunk o' Love" proved to be the most popular, rocketing to number one on the pop charts in 1959. RCA even managed to release a "golden hits" record, and Elvis was not even twenty-five years old! Col. Parker had arranged for a movie deal on a film that would capitalize on Elvis' military service. When he was discharged, Elvis had a contract to film a picture titled *G.I. Blues*.

The title was apt. Elvis was a G.I. and he had the blues. He wrote mournful letters to his friends and his father about how much he missed home. The emotional wound he felt over losing his mother would not heal. When out on furlough, Elvis filled the void with partying and girls. At some point during his service, likely during one of the army's periodic drill-to-you-drop sessions, a sergeant supplied amphetamines to Elvis. Without giving it a thought, Elvis immediately took to the drugs and found that they helped to ease the boredom of life in the service as well as the pain he felt over the loss of his mother.

Vernon's behavior in Germany added to Elvis' distress. Dee Stanley, the wife of an army sergeant, sent Elvis a dinner invitation. Elvis felt like it would be awkward to have dinner with an older married woman, but he could not really refuse the wife of a superior officer. Elvis asked Vernon to go instead. It turned out that Dee was separating from her husband at the time, and Vernon developed a romance with her. To Elvis, it was almost blasphemy for Vernon to take a new girlfriend so soon, or ever, after the death of Gladys. But there was no stopping the relationship and it soon became public knowledge. Meanwhile, Elvis soon found himself in a controversial relationship, and it was one he worried would end his career.

On September 13, 1959, an airman friend of Elvis' introduced the singer-soldier to a fourteen-year-old girl named Priscilla Beaulieu. She'd been born as Priscilla Ann Wagner, in Brooklyn, just a few weeks after the German surrender in WWII. Priscilla's mother, Ann, was just nineteen years old at the time of Priscilla's birth. Just six months later, with the war in the Pacific now ended as well, Priscilla's father died in a plane crash while on his way back home. Three years after the tragedy, Ann remarried an officer in the Air Force named Paul Beaulieu and he adopted Priscilla. Ann and Paul would go on to have five more children, and they all got used to moving around as the Air Force dictated.

Priscilla disliked all the moving, as it caused difficulties in her social life. She had just settled into a junior high school in Texas when her stepfather got orders to transfer to Weisbaden, West Germany. The move left her feeling lonely and fragile, something that Elvis must have recognized in her when they met. Losing his mother seemed to cause Elvis to regress to a teenager himself, and he stammered shyly when he met Priscilla.

Elvis Presley was twenty-four years old, a decade older than Priscilla, when they began a romantic relationship.

## Chapter Eight

# G.I. Blues

On January 1, 1953, a twenty-nine-year-old singer-songwriter named Hank Williams died in the backseat of a car on his way to a show in Canton, Ohio. For his whole life, Williams suffered in pain from a spinal condition. Every song he wrote, whether it was country, rock n' roll, or rockabilly, contained the rhythm of his genius. Fifty-five of the songs he penned made it into Billboard's top ten charts, and he all but invented country music for the radio. Hank's muses sang the same tune as his sirens, and his alcoholism and pill-popping caused erratic behavior. He missed shows, and he got fired from the Grand ol' Opry.

At some point late in 1952, he got into a bar fight and the beating he took might have caused slow hemorrhages in his arteries and brain. The combination of drugs, alcohol, and the fight seem to have killed him. When his body was returned to Alabama for burial, the shocked crowd performed the Hank William's gospel song "I Saw the Light" in his honor.

On December 12, 1957, Jerry Lee Lewis, the regent of rock n' roll while the Army kept Elvis, married his 13-year-old cousin, Myra Gale Brown. Lewis, 22, kept the marriage a secret because he knew what his fans, and Myra's daddy, would do if they found out. When Myra's father learned of the wedding, which was legal, he grabbed a rifle and headed to Sun Records. Cooler heads prevailed and Sam Phillips thought that sending Jerry Lee out of the country for a British tour might be a good idea.

Jerry took his new bride with him to Britain, but the presence of his female thirteen-year-old cousin caused reporters to start asking questions. When Myra introduced herself as Jerry Lee's wife, the scandal broke. Fans deserted Jerry Lee, and Myra soon became pregnant with their child. Only one of his songs, "High School Confidential," a soundtrack to a 1958 B-movie, of the same name, about an undercover police officer in a high school, ever got into the top-25 as a rock song. Jerry Lee's drug and alcohol habit contributed to his decline, and the marriage with Myra would later break up.

Elvis knew about both Hank Williams and Jerry Lee Lewis and the dangers of the fast life for celebrities. For much of his time in the army, Elvis obsessed over the direction of his musical career. The way in which Jerry Lee Lewis lost his career, in a relationship similar to the one Elvis found himself developing with Priscilla, concerned Presley. This concern, however, did not stop Elvis from pursuing her.

Priscilla and Elvis spent much of their time talking, especially after Priscilla's stepfather imposed a curfew after Elvis kept Priscilla out too late on a date. Priscilla, like nearly every other junior-high-aged American girl, developed an infatuation with Elvis. She received nasty letters from jealous girls across the Atlantic and recognized that she was living out a popular fantasy by dating Elvis.

Elvis understood that the age gap made his relationship with Priscilla inappropriate. It's not clear what the extent of their physical relationship was, although both Priscilla and Elvis seemed to think that they had discovered a moral loophole by engaging in sexual activities other than penetrative intercourse. What Elvis seemed to want was to find a pretty teenager, lock her in emotionally, and then have her stay pure and faithful to him while he messed around with other women. Eventually, Elvis and Col. Tom Parker figured Priscilla would turn 18 and then they could get married in the light of the public eye.

By the time Elvis met Priscilla, he had passed the halfway point in his military service. Discharge came in early March of 1960. While he could not keep news of his relationship to Priscilla quiet, he was able to create a sense of plausible deniability involving his physical relationship with her. Elvis never intended to remain faithful to his young girlfriend, but he did intend to marry her when she turned 18 and then the public could find out.

Meanwhile, the Army made Elvis a sergeant and then discharged him. On his last day in Germany, Elvis gave Priscilla his army jacket and requested that she send him letters on pink paper. Sergeant Presley returned stateside on March 3, 1960, at Fort Dix, New Jersey. His fans greeted him with cheers, fireworks, and a brass band. Two years before, when Elvis submitted himself for physical inspection on his first day in the Army, the pictures of him in his underwear showed that he still carried a little baby fat. Two years of army life had physically transformed Elvis. Trim and muscular, in his physical prime at the age of twenty-five, he now had the looks of a Hollywood leading man. That's what Col. Tom Parker intended for Elvis to be.

As Parker had predicted, Elvis' stint in the army won over most of his conservative critics. A Tennessee senator, Estes Kefauver, read out a prepared statement in praise of Elvis. Also, as Parker had predicted, the press swarmed around Elvis looking for pictures. Parker blocked access wherever he could; any reporter wanting a picture of Elvis needed to pony up thousands of dollars.

Parker liked playing the role of movie mogul; he made more money than as a concert promoter, and he had Hollywood agents and movie producers catering to him. Col. Tom Parker did not seem to care much for women; he barely saw his wife and did not like to be touched even by the prettiest of girls. He liked being treated like a big shot, and the movie business allowed him to play that role.

Rock n' roll evolved into something new while Elvis served in the army. Chuck Berry's "Johnny B. Goode," released in 1958, featured a stripped-down sound with just drums, Berry's vocals, and an electric guitar. Along with Berry, Little Richard broke the color line in popular rock music. Berry's fame in 1958 came in second only to Elvis, and Little Richard performed "Long Tall Sally" and "Good Golly, Miss Molly" in 1956 and 1958 to enthusiastic audiences. Richard, a flamboyant dresser with pancake makeup on his cheeks and liner on his eye lashes, didn't threaten husbands and boyfriends in the way that Elvis did.

Because of Parker's movie obsession, Elvis would sit out most of the changes that the early 1960's brought to rock n' roll. The first movie that Elvis made after army life was a picture about army life. The title was *G.I. Blues* and Elvis played Tulsa Mclean, a soldier in the army with an ambition to open a nightclub. When Elvis-as-Mclean performed a song. A displaced patron put on a record by Elvis Presley and interrupted Mclean's performance. No doubt the audience appreciated the winking inside joke.

Mclean figured that the best way to raise money for his nightclub was to try and turn his good looks and lady-killing charm into some quick cash. Luckily, his army buddy, nicknamed Dynamite, will take a large bet that Mclean will not be able to sexually

*Elvis (right) and producer Hal Wallis relax between scenes of "G.I. Blues." The background is filmed in Germany; the rest will be filmed in the States.*

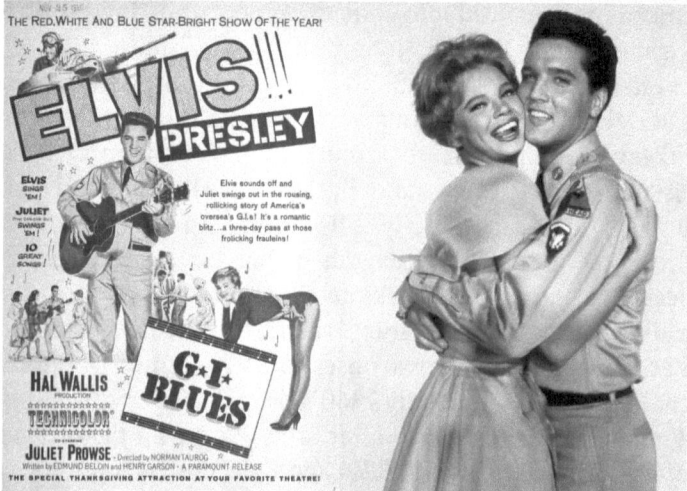

A promotional sign for *G.I. Blues* (bottom left). Elvis and co-star Juliet Prowse (bottom right).

seduce a notoriously standoffish dancer named Lili (played by Juliet Prowse.) In the process Mclean falls in love and a romance develops between the two.

The film featured a juvenile plot, but Elvis got to show off his post-service physique and golden tan . The song-and-dance routines received good reviews.

Also released in 1960 was the film *Flaming Star* featuring Elvis as Pacer Burton, a man with a Kiowa mother and a white father. When fighting breaks out between white settlers and the Native Americans who were indigenous to the land, Pacer joins the Native side. Pacer's brother, also half-Kiowa and half-white, joins the whites.

A dramatic screenplay and a well-known director (Don Siegel) were somehow not quite enough to make the movie a draw for most audiences. Still, a shirtless Elvis looked trim and tan on the movie poster. Also, his love interest in the movie, Roslyn Pierce, was played by Barbra Eden (more famous for playing the scantily clad genie on the hit show *I Dream of Genie*) gave the men in the audience a pretty face to look at. While not quite a flop, Flaming Star did not gross nearly as well as *G.I. Blues*. The Elvis "brand," it seemed, was for campy musicals.

In addition to being the year that Elvis returned stateside, became a civilian, and started cranking out movies, 1960 featured a presidential election. Dwight D. Eisenhower, elected in 1952, already served two terms, leaving an opening for the Republican candidate. So, the Republican Party ran Eisenhower's vice-president, Richard Milhouse Nixon.

At the time, Nixon was just forty-seven years old. A WWII navy veteran with eight years of experience as the vice president, he seemed like a natural candidate to succeed Eisenhower as the Republican Party's choice. The Democrats selected John F. Kennedy (JFK) to run as their presidential candidate.

JFK, at forty-three, was even younger than Nixon. The 1960 presidential election, reflecting a new postwar youth culture, featured the lowest combined age of presidential candidates in American history. Although both men were young by presidential political standards, Kennedy appealed more to the youth vote. He'd served as a naval shipman in WWII, and had behaved heroically (even if he embellished the story), after a Japanese torpedo sunk his ship off of the Solomon Islands.

JFK's father, Joseph Patrick Kennedy Sr., made a fortune in the liquor business and aspired to have his eldest son, Joe Kennedy Jr., be president of the United States. WWII claimed Joe Kennedy Jr.'s life, however, and JFK inherited his father's expectations. By 1960, JFK was already defined by ambition and tragedy.

Many people would not vote for JFK because he was Irish Catholic. Some voters rejected Catholic candidates under the auspice that a Catholic president might be controlled by the papacy in Vatican City. As a Quaker, Richard Nixon seemed equally suspicious to many traditional protestants, so Nixon could not fully capitalize on any anti-Catholic prejudice.

The election featured the first televised presidential debate, with most viewers believing that the telegenic JFK won. Between 1956 and 1960, Hawaii and Alaska had been added as states, making the 1960 contest the first election where fifty states participated. JFK won by the slimmest of margins, and maybe only because of some suspicious irregularities, and took office in 1961. With his beautiful and fashionable wife, Jackie Kennedy, by his side, JFK delivered one of the most memorable lines of any presidential inaugural speech. "Ask not what your country can do for you," he said, "ask what you can do for your country."

During the 1960 election season, Rome, Italy hosted the summer Olympics. A sweet-natured eighteen-year-old boxer from Louisville, Kentucky named Cassius Clay won a gold medal in the light-heavyweight division. Soon after, Clay turned

Hope Lange took on her role in *Wild in the Country* after an unsuccessful audition for Maria in *West Side Story*.

professional and began to bulk up to take on the heavyweight division.

Meanwhile, Col. Tom Parker was determined to keep Elvis in the movies, and even more determined to make as much money as possible off Elvis the actor. Parker enjoyed bamboozling the movie producer Hal Willis, and at one point he convinced Willis to buy hundreds of thousands of Elvis photographs to sell for fans. Parker gave the printing job to a friend of his, at a six-hundred-percent mark-up from the industry standard and took a nice kickback for himself. Parker felt as if Paramount studios underpaid Elvis for both *King Creole* and *G.I. Blues* and he wanted to balance the ledger by overcharging Wallis for Elvis in the future.

Although audiences seemed to show a predilection for watching Elvis in breezy musicals, Parker and Elvis still thought that Elvis had a chance to be the next Marlon Brando or James Dean. In June of 1961, Paramount released *Wild in the Country* with Elvis channeling James Dean as a rebellious, immature, two-fisted twenty-five-year-old writer named Glenn Tyler.

In self-defense, Tyler hurt his drunken brother during a brawl. Nonetheless, Tyler got into trouble with the law and had to serve probation in a peaceful small town under the watch of his uncle. While there, Tyler receives counseling from a beautiful young psychiatrist named Irene Sperry (played by Hope Lange.) The townsfolk don't take to Glenn Tyler, and he becomes the subject of gossip and innuendo, especially about his relationship with Sperry. Nonetheless, Sperry falls in love with her tortured-soul of a patient. Tyler finally goes off to college to pursue his life as an author.

Elvis sang a few obligatory songs in the movie, which seemed out of place in what most critics and movie-goers thought was a woeful melodrama. The movie made less than what it cost to produce, something which alarmed Col. Tom Parker and the movie's producers. In 1961, Elvis the actor was just not the big draw that Elvis the singer had been just five years before.

Additionally, audiences could just never quite see Elvis as the character's that he played. Whenever he was on screen, he was still Elvis Presley, and his acting skills could never persuade audiences of anything else. The people wanted to see Elvis in fun musicals, playing the guitar and wooing a pretty starlet, but not doing much else. After *Wild in the Country* that's what Elvis would give his audiences from then on.

## Chapter Nine

# Movie Star

Col. Tom Parker had a big new idea for a movie: Elvis needed to be in Hawaii. Hawaii's natural beauty made a deep impression on Parker during the time he spent there in the service. The tropical islands, now a U.S. state, would provide the perfect backdrop to Elvis as a leading man. Parker also wanted to get Elvis off the contiguous forty-eight states, and out in the Pacific, to keep him away from RCA. RCA's executives wanted Elvis in the studio, recording hit song after hit song, but Parker worried that such an approach would create Elvis fatigue in audiences. Parker liked the moving picture business better anyway; Elvis the actor proved to be easier to manage than Elvis the singer.

Although Parker had a few ideas for a plotline, Wallis decided just to make a movie about good-looking people in a beautiful place. By the time anyone noticed that the movie had no real plot, the picture would be over. Elvis' character in the film, Chad Gates, returns home to Hawaii after a stint in the army. Once home, Gates faces pressure from his mother to take over the family fruit-growing business but he just wants to roam the islands as a tour guide, play the guitar, and sing. So, Gates does that instead.

*Blue Hawaii* came in second at the box office during its opening week in November and was promoted by some of the best movie-posters in Hollywood history, but did little to enhance Elvis' reputation as an actor. Audiences did not want to see Elvis as a dramatic hero; they wanted to see him fall in love, and then sing and dance about falling in love.

In 1962, the Elvis movie genre probably reached its nadir with *Girls! Girls! Girls!.* In this film, released in October, Elvis plays a fishing guide named Ross Carpenter who works on a boat called the Westwind in (where else?) Hawaii. When his boss decides to retire, Ross develops a dream of owning the boat but can't afford

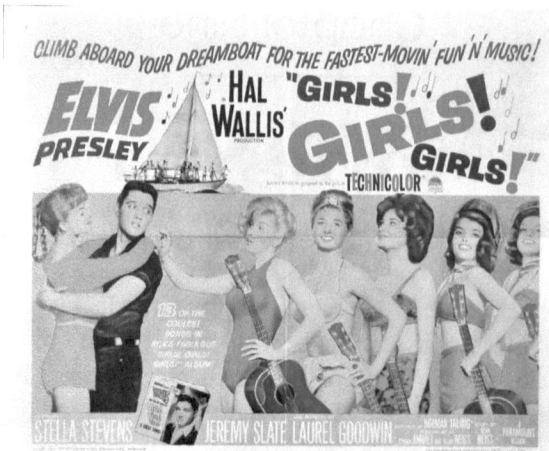

This movie was marketed as a "dreamboat of a drama." and delivered exactly what Elvis fans wanted - a love story with lots of singing.

it. Meanwhile, two women compete for the affections of Ross. One of the women is named Laurel and the other is named Robin. Ross ends up punching out the new owner of the Westwind.

Oh, and Ross Carpenter can also sing and regularly performs in tropical nightclubs. In the movie, Carpenter sings the song "Return to Sender." This became one of the biggest hits that Elvis ever produced for a movie soundtrack and it went number one in the UK and became a number two hit in the United States. Elvis never looked better than he did singing that hit in the movie. Lean, tan, dressed in black, and in full control of his dance moves, Elvis gave the audience what it came to see. *Girls! Girls! Girls!* did not make much sense, but it did make a nice profit at the box office.

Also in 1962, Elvis played in *Kid Galahad*, a remake of a 1937 fight film. Elvis played Walter Gulick, a mechanic who (you guessed it) needs money and ends up at a boxing camp in the Catskills. Gulick takes on a job as the sparring partner for a pro, and during the first sparring match he demonstrates a talent for taking punches. Gulick emerges unscathed (the scene with Gulick taking shots to the face, no doubt, concerned many in Elvis' female fan base.) After a few rounds of taking a drubbing, Gulick uncorks one right hand and knocks the pro cold.

Seeing an opportunity, Gulick's new trainer, Lew Nyack (played memorably by Charles Bronson) decides to turn his prodigy professional. But the mob wants Gulick to take a dive and Nyack needs the money. Gulick doesn't take a dive after all and wins his fights. Oh, and Gulick woos a cute young woman along the way. He also sings some songs, including "I Got Lucky" along with some help from a spontaneous, but rhythmic, crew of background singers.

The hits just kept coming. In 1963, Paramount released *It Happened at the World's Fair*, where Elvis played a crop-duster named Mike Edwards who needs money, or he will lose his crop-duster. While at the World's fair, Mike develops a friendship with a young Asian girl who can't find her uncle. Meanwhile, Mike develops a crush on an unfriendly nurse. He and the little girl plot to make the nurse change her mind and fall in love with Mike. At one point, Mike decides to deliberately get an injury so he can visit the nurse. The plot involved paying a young boy for a reciprocal kick in the shin. The boy, played by Kurt Russell in his film debut, delivered the kick. Mike duly made a trip to the nurse.

At this point, Elvis' movies all seemed to fall into the same plot pattern. Elvis plays a handsome ne'er-do-well in need of money, he then finds a novel way to make the money, woos a woman, sometimes delivers a punch to the deserving chin of a bad

*Kissin' Cousins* was filmed in Los Angeles. Filmmakers used the San Berandino Mountains to replicate the mountainous setting of the movie.

guy, and sings a few songs along the way. After *It Happened at the World's Fair*, there seemed to be a plan by Paramount to put Elvis in the weirdest situations, with the strangest plots, imaginable. This may be how *Kissin' Cousins*, released in 1964, got made.

Elvis plays two characters in this movie. The first is Josh Morgan, an officer in the Air Force. The second is Jodie Tatum, a hillbilly who lives in the Great Smoky Mountains of Tennessee. The two men find out they are identical cousins, but, as luck would have it, Josh's hair is black while Jodie's is blonde.

Josh Morgan as an Air Force Officer is commissioned to help convince a group of Tennessee hill-folk to allow the Air Force to build a missile base on their property. When an Air Force caravan travels up the mountains, they are greeted with a hail of rifle fire. Elvis-as-Josh is sent up to try and talk to the shooters, only to be confronted by two pretty but hard-bitten and well-armed mountain women. They seem shocked to see Josh, and when Jodie, who has blonde hair, steps out from behind a bush Josh can see why. Jodie is Josh's blonde doppelganger.

Elvis and Anita Wood, one of his previous girlfriends, 1960.

Jodie, wearing a red-checked flannel shirt says "What are you doing with my face?"

It turns out that Josh, Jodie, and the mountain women are all cousins!

After that Elvis engages in some romance with his cousins and sings a couple of songs about how that's okay. "Kissin' Cousins" was the feature song on the soundtrack and remains one of the few rock n' roll songs in praise of incest. The main song-and-dance routine features Elvis in two roles, one in a military uniform and the other in a gaudy country-and-western get up. It turns out that Pappy Tatum, the owner of the property, doesn't really care if the Air Force builds a missile launching pad on his land, he just wants to make sure that his moonshine still will be safe. When the Air Force guarantees that, Pappy gives them permission to build.

Elvis movies may have been campy, but Americans needed a diversion more than ever. The years between 1960 and 1964 brought more political turbulence than the end of WWII. Upon taking office as president, JFK adopted a posture of aggression toward the Soviet Union. His get-tough approach, plus an overreliance on advice from the Central Intelligence Agency (CIA), led to the Bay of Pigs debacle in Cuba on April 4, 1961.

In 1959, a young and bearded revolutionary named Fidel Castro led a rebellion of jungle guerillas against the dictatorship of Fulgencio Batista. Castro commanded only a small number of rebels, but Batista's long period of brutal rule left him with few supporters. Not long after taking power, Castro declared himself to be a Communist. Then he seized the assets of wealthy Cubans and kicked them off the island. Most of the Cuban exiles came to the United States.

A hostile Communist government just ninety miles south of Florida now confronted the U.S. government and military. The CIA's plan to remedy the problem, signed off by JFK, involved training those Cuban exiles in military invasion tactics and then sending them back to Cuba to engage in an armed overthrow of the new Castro regime. The United States military was under strict orders not to engage the Cubans directly, only to watch as the invasion occurred.

On April 17, 1961, 1,500 Cuban exiles, called Brigade 2506, landed on Cuba's beaches. Two days later, Castro's government forces killed and captured a little more than three hundred of the invading exiles and held 1,189 of them as prisoners. Kennedy, humiliated by the debacle, started negotiations for the return of prisoners. Over a year and a half later, Cuba and the United States reached a deal where the prisoners could return to the United

States in exchange for a massive payment of medicine and food.

The invasion turned into such a debacle that it worsened the already strained relationship between the United States and the Soviet Union. Just a few months later, in August of 1961, the Soviets in East Berlin built a wall down the middle of Germany's capital city. For Khrushchev and the Politburo (Soviet cabinet), Berlin had become a public relations problem. East Berliners frequently crossed over in huge numbers to the Western sector to enjoy a better quality of life. The Soviets, it seemed, were effective at fighting wars and building rockets, but not effective at providing a decent quality of life for ordinary people. Guards on the eastern side of the wall were given standing orders to shoot and kill anyone trying to breach the wall. The Berlin Wall was the metaphorical Iron Curtain, a concept dubbed by Winston Churchill during WWII, made manifest.

Relations kept getting worse. Since the United States kept missiles in Western Europe, close enough to hit Russia, the Soviets were nervous about future attacks. They did not have any missiles capable of reaching the U.S. to fight back. The Soviets became eager to create military parity. Khrushchev and the Communist Party in Russia took advantage of the opportunity presented by the Bay of Pigs Invasion by installing ICBMs in Cuba. On October 14, 1962, U-2 spy planes in the service of the CIA took pictures of the missiles.

The Colonel was all about power and keeping it. He was ruthless when creating contracts and was always present to make sure things went his way.

JFK could not allow the Soviets to station missiles so close to U.S. soil, but he also could not invade a sovereign country like Cuba without causing a serious escalation of tensions that could lead to large-scale nuclear war. For nine days, the United States and the Soviet Union risked WWIII in a face-off over the missiles. Finally, Khrushchev agreed to remove the missiles in exchange for a U.S. promise to remove similar missiles from Eastern Europe. Khrushchev never recovered his reputation in the Communist Party, and the Politburo soon deposed him into a comfortable, but forced, retirement.

Kennedy proved to be a force in popular culture for many of the same reasons that Elvis was; he had a voice easily mimicked, and good looks that attracted the attention of women everywhere. In a bid to create international goodwill, JFK created the Peace Corps even as he gradually intensified the U.S. presence to support French recolonization efforts in Vietnam. In 1961, at a speech given at Rice University in Texas, Kennedy announced the seemingly far-fetched plan for NASA to put astronauts on the moon by the end of the decade. In June of 1963, he gave a famous speech at the Brandenburg Gate in West Berlin where he declared solidarity with Berliners while at the same time calling for a peaceful solution to end the Cold War.

Increasingly, the civil rights movement became the central focus of domestic politics and culture in the United States. Kennedy appointed Thurgood Marshall, among many other black justices, to a federal judgeship. He also sent federal marshals into the deep south to provide protection for the black Americans, known as "Freedom Riders," who refused to sit in segregated sections on public buses. With the vigor of a young idealist, Kennedy made an impression on nearly every sector of society. College students, especially, seemed to support his political aims.

Then, on November 22, 1963, at 12:30 PM in Dallas, Texas, an unhinged former marine named Lee Harvey Oswald shot JFK in the head. Oswald shot from a distance with a high-powered rifle, and a bystander named Abraham Zapruder filmed it with an 8mm color recorder. Elvis felt the impact of JFK's death personally. As the world's most famous entertainer, he had met President Kennedy in 1962 when Kennedy made a personal visit to Graceland.

Although Elvis rarely expressed political views, he was supportive of Kennedy's integration efforts and had been impressed by JFK during their lone interaction. It was at this time, with the nation in mourning, that a new invasive threat emerged. The Beatles were coming.

## Chapter Ten

# The Beatles are Coming

In 1956, John Lennon, then a sixteen-year-old student at Quarry Bank High School in Liverpool, England, formed a rock band with a few friends. A year later, a fifteen-year-old named Paul McCartney and his friend George Harrison attended one of Lennon's shows and were impressed. Harrison played guitar and tried to audition, but Lennon did not want to associate with kids who were younger. Eventually, Harrison found a time when Lennon was a captive audience, during a ride on a public bus, and riffed off a guitar solo. Impressed, Lennon hired Harrison to play guitar for his band.

By 1959, Lennon's original band dissolved, and he enrolled at the Liverpool College of Art. He formed a new band, named Johnny and the Moondogs, with Harrison and McCartney. All three were guitarists, however, and could only put on shows whenever they could convince a drummer to join them. They eventually welcomed a sub-par percussionist named Pete Best. One of Lennon's chums at the art school, named Stuart Sutcliffe, joined up to play the Bass guitar. Sutcliffe had been a fan of Buddy Holly and the Crickets, so he suggested the Beatles as a name for the musical troupe. For a while, the four went by the Silver Beatles but quickly changed to just the Beatles.

In the summer of 1960, the Beatles acquired a manager named Allan Williams, who booked them to play clubs in the seediest part of Hamburg, West Germany. The Beatles first paying stint was, more or less, to be the house band for a brothel. Eventually, the Beatles kicked around various clubs in Hamburg and eventually made their way back to Liverpool, England, where they started playing in an underground cellar called The Cavern Club. By that time, the Beatles had played nightly for so long that they were one of the best-rehearsed rock bands on the planet.

Soon enough, the Beatles became a local happening. Posters advertising their shows went up across the city. In 1961, Brian Epstein, a young music store manager in England, kept hearing rumors about a four-man band that played in various clubs around Liverpool. On November 9, Epstein decided to check the band out for himself during a midday performance at The Cavern Club.

The Beatles packed the house and had all the young people dancing during sets. In between songs, the bandmates entertained the crowd with witty banter that left Epstein charmed and besotted. He met the Beatles after the concert and over the next few months developed a rapport with the members. In early 1962, Epstein signed a contract to manage the Beatles.

The Beatles became popular enough in Liverpool that contacts close with the band had already reached out to Ed Sullivan. However, in 1962, the band was still too obscure for Sullivan to take a chance on them. Epstein tried to create a new path for the band: they needed to get out of Hamburg and Liverpool and start seeking more exposure. It took a little while to disentangle the Beatles from previous contracts, but eventually Epstein signed the Beatles with Electric and Music Industries (EMI), a premier British record label controlled by producer George Martin.

Martin brought the band in for a recording session at Abbey Road in June of 1962 and immediately disliked the drumming of Pete Best. The other bandmates and Epstein also recognized Best as a weak link and agreed to replacing him. Epstein then courted drummer Ringo Starr, who had been playing for Rory Storm and the Hurricanes, and completed the Beatles line up that fans would come to call the Fab Four: John Lennon, Paul McCartney, George Harrison, and Ringo Starr.

By the end of 1962, the Beatles worked through their Hamburg contract, and there would be no more playing in bars and brothels. They started 1963 with a pact that all members would sing, at least a little, on their albums. Lennon and McCartney would write the songs. Epstein convinced the group to clean up their stage act. They needed to stop smoking and cursing while on stage; they needed to grow up a little.

In February of 1963, the Beatles released a ten-song album titled *Please Please Me*. The album included four singles that had already been released to the public. The title track came out just a little bit before the album and topped the UK's popular-music charts. Word of the band's new sound started to drift across the Atlantic. Epstein recognized that the vastly larger American audience could propel the Beatles into a new realm of stardom. Untold profits could be made.

As was the case with Elvis, most fans heard the music before getting to know the musicians. Fans who shimmied to "Please Please Me" were delighted to see the Beatles, or the "four lads from Liverpool," on the UK television programs. The Beatles delighted in joking with each other, and their youthful shenanigans appealed to Europeans weary of war and the politics of the Iron Curtain. Their popularity grew with the release of every single and album and every public appearance made their fans more enthusiastic.

On October 13, 1963, the Beatles played live on Sunday night at the London Palladium, which was the United Kingdom's version of *The Ed Sullivan Show*. Not only did fifteen million viewers watch the performance, but young people everywhere seemed to be constantly talking about the band. No one had drawn attention like this since Elvis, and the UK's press declared "Beatlemania" to be a true phenomenon.

When the Beatles finally came to the United States in November, of 1963, they were still virtually anonymous. Walter Cronkite, the CBS nightly news anchor whom Americans trusted for his reporting, planned to air an interview with the Fab Four. A five-minute piece with Mike Wallace had aired just a few days before. However, JFK's assassination made a story about the Beatles look frivolous at the time. A nation in mourning was not interested in Beatlemania. A few months later, Cronkite thought Americans might be ready for a lighter story about a band and aired an interview with the Fab Four.

This got the attention of Ed Sullivan, who called Cronkite and inquired about "the bugs, or whatever they call themselves." Cronkite vouched for the youngsters, and Sullivan booked them for a show on February 7, 1964. The Beatles were back in Liverpool at the time, and their departure for America caused a stir with their fans; several thousands showed John, Paul, George, and Ringo off at the airport. A similar reception greeted them when their plane landed in the United States. Beatlemania had finally arrived.

Finally, Ed Sullivan, who had once been reluctant to book Elvis too, decided the time had come for the Beatles to appear on his show. The American press steadily proclaimed that "The Beatles are Coming" or "The British Invasion!" American audiences had not been whipped up into such a frenzy of anticipation since Elvis appeared on the *Steve Allen Show* so many years ago to sing to a hound dog. The Beatles, however, would be subject to no such humiliation. Rock n' roll music no longer carried the same shock value, and George, Paul, John, and Ringo didn't shake their hips.

On February 9. 1964 the Beatles debuted to an American audience by playing their hit "I Want to Hold your Hand." The three guitarists, John, Paul, and George took center stage while Ringo was set up behind them with his drum set. John Lennon sang the lead vocal. All four wore suits, but looked like rakish choir boys with their long unkempt hair and occasionally smirking expressions. When Ed Sullivan's cameraman panned to the audience, he picked up footage of women and girls shaking in borderline hysteria.

The Nielsen ratings numbers did not lie. Thirty-four percent of Americans, comprising twenty-three million homes, tuned in to the broadcast. Nielsen ratings did not sort for age, but it's almost certain that a vastly higher percentage of people who were twenty-five or younger watched the Beatles. At the time, the audience was the largest that the Nielsen ratings system had ever recorded. Along with JFK's assassination, the Beatles introductory performance on *The Ed Sullivan Show* defined the experience of a generation of school kids.

The Beatles sang right through some of the negative reviews they received from a press. Who cared what those old squares thought anyways? They played at a packed house in Carnegie Hall, and then went back on *The Ed Sullivan Show* on February 22nd where they played the upbeat and soon-to-be iconic "Twist and Shout" before an audience almost as large as the one that watched their first performance.

During this time period, Elvis was not quite forgotten, but he no longer possessed the raw force of rock n' roll stardom that he once had. Americans twenty-five and under, who made up the majority of music consumers, clearly saw the Beatles as the standard-bearers for youth culture. Elvis continued making movies, and the first picture to be released during Beatlemania went by the title of *Viva Las Vegas* which came out in May of 1964.

Many Elvis fans consider *Viva Las Vegas* to be his best movie, not in the least because the actress Ann-Margret proved to be such an alluring love interest. Unlike in previous movies, where Elvis played an everyman, *Viva Las Vegas* featured Elvis as Lucky Jackson, a glamorous racecar driver who had made his way to Vegas to race his Maserati in a Grand Prix. Upon arrival in Nevada, Jackson's engine broke down and he had to raise money for a new one.

Yet, Jackson met a swimming instructor, a vivacious red-head named Rusty Martin (Ann-Margret) who is initially unimpressed by Jackson's attempts to woo her. The musical scene where Jackson plays the guitar in a suit, while Martin does favors for a swimsuit while walking around the pool, is now remembered as one of Hollywood's finest musical numbers. The duet ends with Rusty shoving Jackson off the diving board and into a pool, where he loses the cash he was holding on to. The lost money had been meant for a new engine, so now Jackson took work at the casino

Ann-Margret described her romantic relationship with Elvis as "a force [they] couldn't control."

where Rusty worked, hoping to earn money for the car while also earning the affections of the lady.

Elvis and Ann-Margret made for an engaging couple on-screen, and so it was in real-life. In 1964, Presley was still the most eligible bachelor in the country, and Margret's beauty, personality, and talent broke many a movie-goers heart. The two made for a natural pair, and the romance continued on and off for three years. Many of Elvis' close friends hoped that Elvis would move on from his romance-in-abeyance with Priscilla and just marry Ann-Margret. It was, however, not to be. Elvis still intended to marry Priscilla.

*Viva Las Vegas* certainly made money, earning back nine times its production costs. In 1964, the Beatles dominated the rock n' roll music scene, but even the Fab Four could not ignore this kind of profit. As big as the Beatles were, they were following a pattern first established by Col. Tom Parker and Elvis Presley. They got their break on Ed Sullivan, released some big albums, and then went into the movies.

As was always the case with an Elvis movie, *Viva Las Vegas* the movie was accompanied by a soundtrack that was released as a single. The song "Viva Las Vegas" was released on an LP in 1963 and was played on the radio. It failed to crack the top ten on any pop chart, and there is no evidence that Elvis ever performed it live, but "Viva Las Vegas" lives on as one of Elvis' most iconic songs because it fits perfectly with so many movies and television shows that use Vegas as a location.

In July of 1964, with Beatlemania reaching a crescendo, the movie *A Hard Day's Night* starring the Beatles as themselves, was released as a comedy-musical. The film was made on the cheap, with producers counting on the Fab Four, rather than a plot, to attract moviegoers, and it made a nice profit. The Beatles may have been the biggest thing going in 1964, but it took four of them to walk in Elvis' footsteps.

## Chapter Eleven

# Harum Scarum

At some point during the spring of 1960, Nel Dankers-van Kujik, a homemaker living in the Netherlands, picked up a copy of a woman's magazine while she waited to have her hair styled. The magazine contained a feature about Elvis Presley, and there, with him, was a rotund man named Col. Tom Parker. Nel recognized Parker; it was her long-lost brother. Col. Tom Parker was once called "Dries" (short for Andres) by his family.

Nel quickly showed the rest of her family the magazine and everyone confirmed that Tom Parker and "Andres" were one and the same. The family had not entirely lost contact with their brother, but the occasional post-card or note was not enough to let them know what he was doing in the United States. Nel and her brothers sent Parker a letter to confirm that Tom Parker, manager of Elvis, and Andres, missing relative, were the same.

Parker received the letter but did not reply until January 31st of 1961. In a nebulous response, he seemed cautious about what the family wanted to know and made some cryptic remarks about why he had left Holland to begin with. Col. Tom Parker seemed less than eager to explore his past. Elvis, then consumed with his entrance into the Army, seemed incurious about his manager. Col. Parker kept money in Elvis' pocket, but beyond that Elvis seemed content to assume that Parker was a former Army officer from West Virginia.

Parker's family did come to visit him in the United States, but Parker was curt and the visit short. He seemed to want few connections to his old life. But there were other aspects of Parker's history, that became intertwined with Elvis' career.

In addition to *Kissin' Cousins* and *Viva Las Vegas*, one more Elvis movie came out in 1964. The film, titled *Roustabout*, featured Elvis as a down-and-out singer named Charlie Rogers who takes

Raquel Welch admits she had a crush on Elvis as a teenageer. However, the crush wore off as they worked together. She felt he wasn't as rebellious and sassy as his on-stage persona in real life.

a job working in a carnival. It was another film that Hal Wallis directed, and even though Wallis hated Parker, the movie was a nod to Parker's early life as a carnival barker. Parker reacted with feigned indignation; if his life was to inspire a movie, then he should be paid for it.

The movie was traditional Elvis-movie fare; Elvis plays a two-fisted ne'er-do-well with more passion than brains. Elvis-as-Charlie-Rogers gets into a fistfight with some college boys, spends a night in jail, and gets into a motorcycle race the next day. A beauty named Maggie Morgan (Barbara Stanwyck) rehabilitates Rogers and invites him to work as a "roustabout" for her failing carnival. Charlie Rogers finds himself caught in a romance between different women, then makes it big as a singer, and makes enough money to save the struggling carnival.

*Roustabout* may be most notable because Raquel Welch, then just 24 years old, made her film debut. Welch had been a teenager when Elvis first made it big in the 1950's, and like most American girls of the era she had nursed a crush on Elvis. It appears that no relationship formed between the two, however, as Elvis was already tangled up with both Priscilla and Ann-Margret. Welch later said that an entourage always surrounded Elvis, so he was hard to talk with.

Although the movie was not considered to be Elvis' best effort, the album that made up the film's soundtrack went to number one that October, just before the assassination of JFK and the invasion of the Beatles. More than any other film, *Roustabout* proved that

*Roustabout* was Barbara Stanwych's 77th Hollywood film. She was surprised to be offered a role in an Elvis film, but took it as she thought it would be fun to create a film for a younger audience.

Elvis was trapped in a paradox; his movies and music made more money than ever, but the movies were so low-brow that Elvis often felt as if making them was the equivalent of singing to a hound dog, over and over, on the *Steve Allen Show*.

Parker's behavior became increasingly erratic, even irrational. Parker decided to have Elvis buy the U.S.S. Potomac, recently decommissioned by the Navy, for $55,000. Supposedly, the buy was designed as a homage to Elvis' respect for FDR, who had used the ship as a governmental based throughout much of WWII. Parker liked nothing more than to be treated like a big shot, and he thought that if Elvis purchased the boat, and gave it to the March of Dimes, then this would be a big publicity coup.

The problem was that the administrators of the March of Dimes, who had not been consulted prior to the purchase, could not conceive of what they were supposed to do with a ship. Surprised and alarmed to hear that they were about to inherit an aircraft carrier, they declined the gift. Parker then tried to hand the ship off to the Coast Guard, but nobody there wanted it either.

Eventually, Parker talked St. Jude Children's hospital, located in Memphis, into take taking the ship. Elvis showed up for the photo opportunity, but he blamed Parker for the debacle and was outwardly angry at the Colonel for perhaps the first time. As Elvis approached age thirty, he was becoming more independent and was increasingly frustrated with the direction of his career.

Elvis could have fired Col. Tom Parker at any time, but he chose not to. Elvis showed little interest in the business of being Elvis; he just showed up in the studio to sing or showed up on set to make movies. So much money flooded in that it did not really seem to matter that Parker took more for his share than what a normal manager would. Also, Parker had pioneered the movie/soundtrack entertainment combo that turned Elvis into a megastar and profit-machine, so it was hard to argue with the Colonel's model.

Elvis' movie production team faced some level of public recrimination for putting Elvis in so many films with cookie-cutter plots. The producers pointed out that the profits from Elvis films allowed for the making of the 1964 film, *Becket*, starring Richard Burton as Thomas Becket and Peter O' Toole as Henry II, an enduring historical drama about the Twelfth century clash between an irascible English king and his equally stubborn archbishop. Movies that impressed the critics only rarely brought in popular audiences. The producer indicated that Elvis had to sing with pretty girls to make money so that the studio could finance higher forms of cinematic art.

Elvis knew his movies could not be considered high art. He had long ago given up on the idea of being the next Marlon Brando, but for a man who had once shook the country when he shook his hips, to be publicly derided for fluff performances hurt his pride. Friends in his entourage started to worry about the increasing numbers of pills that the boss popped. As Elvis neared thirty, late nights, pills, and unhealthy eating caused him to put on some weight. Movie producers knew that Elvis' good looks were what brought in audiences, and so Elvis would crash-diet before arriving on a movie set. He was caught in a cycle.

Friends who were close to Elvis believed he never recovered from the death of his mother. Making matters worse, Elvis could not even rely on his father anymore. In 1960, Vernon had married Dee Stanley, the divorcee' he'd met in Germany. Elvis hated Dee, even if he treated her children kindly, and Dee seemed to have no love for Elvis either. She seemed interested in the Presley money, and became a source of contention between Vernon and Elvis. For a young man who had once relied so much on the affections of his parents, the removal of his family's stability had a deep impact.

Elvis also suffered from overwork, a result of Parker's inexhaustible desire to make as much money off of Elvis as possible.

Shelley Fabares appeared in three Elvis movies, but is best known for her role on *The Donna Reed Show*.

In 1965, three Elvis movies were shown on the big screen, each released just a few months apart. In order of release, they were *Girl Happy* (March 12), *Tickle Me* (June 30), and *Harum Scarum* (December 15). Releasing three movies a year would have been a strain on any actor, and Elvis continued recording soundtracks to the movies, which meant working dual roles.

*Girl Happy* was another musical, this time about a beach party. Elvis played a club singer by the name of Rusty Wells. At the start of the movie, Rusty and his band are playing a club in wintry Chicago while dreaming of a spring vacation in Florida. Then, out of nowhere, the club's owner, named Big Frank, makes the band stay on to play more shows. Rusty and the boys are obviously upset by this, but when Rusty finds out that Big Frank's college-student daughter, Valerie (played by Shelley Fabares) is on her way to Florida, Rusty convinces Big Frank to send the band down to Florida to look after her.

Big Frank, apparently under the impression that a group of young and single musicians are ideal for keeping his beautiful daughter out of trouble, sends the boys down to Florida to sing and look after Valerie. After some hijinks and shenanigans, Rusty and Valerie become sweet on each other and Rusty woos her with a song called "Puppet on a String." At some point, Valerie figures out that her father paid Rusty to look after her, and feeling betrayed, she gets drunk and causes Rusty and the boys to get into a brawl. Everyone goes to jail, but Big Frank finally arrives to sort everything out. Rusty and Valerie are free to fall in love.

Occasionally, an Elvis movie went all-in on an absurd comic premise, and this was the case with *Tickle Me*. The film is now most notable for the fact that the soundtrack included only previously recorded songs. The pace of movie-making and recording had picked up to the point, where including an album with the movie was not feasible. In *Tickle Me*, Elvis plays Lonnie Beale, a rodeo bronc rider who sings on the side. Due to a brawl with a patron, Lonnie lost his job as a club singer and ends up working with the horses at a ranch and weight-loss spa. This means Lonnie works as a cowboy in a place where pretty starlets and models vacationed to lose a few pounds before their roles or modeling gigs.

Lonnie occasionally takes on an impromptu role as a singing cowboy, but his spontaneous singings is an activity not welcomed by the spa's patrons. When one of the starlets, Pam Merritt, heads to a nearby town called Silverado, Lonnie goes with her and then finds out that a hidden treasure is buried somewhere out in the desert. Lonnie and Pam, fail to find the treasure. Even worse, Pam is nearly kidnapped by villains who want information about the treasure's location. Lonnie saves her, and they seem to be falling in love. However, as was frequently the case in an Elvis movie: the problem starts with the main character's fists and gets more complicated when women start throwing themselves at him. Pam, convinced by a misunderstanding that Lonnie is involved with another woman, breaks off the romance.

Lonnie goes back to bronc busting on the rodeo circuit but is too love-sick to concentrate. Pam won't read his letters, putting only "return to sender" on the envelopes. She is haunted, however, by a series of spooks who try to scare her into revealing where the buried treasure is. The spooks turn out to be villains in masks. Lonnie and Pam resolve their differences, uncover the villains' plot, then find the buried treasure and get married.

Yet, it was the third film of 1965 that seemed to wear Elvis, and maybe his audience, completely out. *Harum Scarum* was intended to be a homage to the silent films of Rudolph Valentino, but the plot descended into something more than a farce. The movie poster, featuring Elvis in a turban, was more than a lot of fans could comprehend. Elvis could play bronc riders, lounge singers, farmers, and military men just fine, but it was not clear if his acting range extended to a Middle Eastern adventurer.

Elvis had a high tolerance for low-brow scripts, and always put in a day's work no matter how absurd a picture's premise. But by the time he worked on *Harum Scarum*, he had made 15 movies in five years; he'd started working almost immediately upon returning from the army and the pressure to put out new movies was not just wearing on Elvis but also on the screenwriters, who seemed to be running out of ideas. Audiences could only watch Elvis get into trouble for a fistfight, and then find a way to earn money and woo a pretty girl with his singing, so many times.

The *Harum Scarum* movie trailer promised audiences they would see Elvis performing his new musical hits "Harum Scarum" and "Go East Young Man" while wooing Arabian temptresses and watching dancing girls in the harem. In the picture, Elvis played Johnny Tyrone, an actor going to Arabia to make a movie. While there, a beautiful Arabian woman falls for Johnny, but then is kidnapped by a villain named Sinan. Sinan's plot is to hold the girl until Johnny Tyrone promises to assassinate a king. The plot gets out of hand from there, with one beautiful Arabian woman after another falling in love with Johnny Tyrone and his singing.

Johnny tries to kill the king, but gets caught and is eventually saved by a well-meaning dwarf. This gives Johnny the opportunity to plead his case to the king himself. Luckily, the king believes every word the American actor says, and eventually Johnny and the king join forces against the villains. Johnny and the king defeat the villains, with Johnny winning an epic game of chess against the chief bad guy. Then Johnny marries the king's daughter and takes her and her troupe of dancing girls to Las Vegas for a honeymoon.

## Chapter Twelve

# Spiritualism

On April 30, 1964, Elvis met his new hairdresser, a personable twenty-something named Larry Geller. Elvis had worked with the same hair-stylist for years, and so the change meant that a new person would be breaking into the entourage for the first time since Elvis got out of the Army. Elvis, desperate for real conversation, started asking Geller personal questions.

Geller, it turned out, was a devotee of the New Age "spiritualism" that began to define religious life for many young people in the sixties. When Elvis heard this, he turned the hair styling session with Geller into a psychotherapy session. Elvis listened, and the conversation seemed to fill some need for a depth of conversation that he was missing on the set of his movies. When Elvis talked, he went into detail about the death of his mother and how he felt as if his life had no center anymore. Geller said he would come by the next morning with some books about spiritual philosophy.

When Geller came by the next morning, he brought a stack of New Age literature but the one book that caught Elvis' attention was titled *The Impersonal Life: Autobiography of a Yogi*, which had been published nearly six decades before but had suddenly become hip during the Eastern spiritualist craze brought forth by the college hippies. The author of the book, Joseph Benner, made some nebulous claims about his own life, and the book was filled with cryptic messages that could either be read as divine wisdom or plain silliness depending on who held the book. Elvis felt a connection to the words and saw a new and true friend in Geller.

Elvis asked Geller to bring him more books like *The Impersonal Life*. Suddenly, Elvis' hairdresser had become Elvis' spiritual guide to the New Age. The male entourage, all those bodyguards and hangers-on known as the Memphis Mafia, resented Geller's sudden influence. However, for Elvis, that was the point. He felt a need to make a connection with someone new, and Geller happened to be in a position where he could break through into a one-on-one conversation with him.

While on this spiritual and intellectual journey, Elvis made both *Girl Happy* and *Spinout*. Neither film seemed to reflect the deep questions that Elvis found himself trying to answer through the Eastern spiritualist books he read. Col. Parker turned fifty-five in June of 1964, and in interviews made it clear that Elvis would continue to perform in a way that brought in the money. Elvis and Parker rarely saw each other, and Parker was not the kind of man who would converse for hours about hippie philosophy. Parker may have saved Elvis, however, from making a spectacle of himself. The Beatles, too, embraced Eastern New Age spiritualism and their public pronouncements on philosophy and vegetarianism often came off as elitist and self-important.

In his correspondence with Priscilla, Elvis expressed a desire to have her meet Geller. At the same time, Elvis felt undercut by one of his friends, Johnny Rivers. Rivers had been an on-again and off-again member of the entourage for several years, and while he liked playing guitar with Elvis and the boys, he harbored his own ambitions for fame. In 1959, Chuck Berry released a toe-tapping song with a strong guitar riff titled "Memphis."

Rivers knew that Elvis planned to put out his own version of "Memphis" in 1964. Rivers kept his plans to himself and recorded a new version of "Memphis" in secret. When it came out in the summer of 1964, fans loved it, and Rivers earned an appearance on Dick Clark's American Bandstand. Elvis and the Memphis Mafia all cursed Rivers for scooping Elvis. Presley stopped inviting Johnny Rivers over.

When Elvis did release a new album, in the form of *Such a Night*, his fans barely noticed and the LP sold in numbers usually expected for third-raters. Col. Tom Parker, alarmed at the loss of revenue, met personally with Elvis. Parker accused his singer of being on a "religious kick," and the accusation infuriated Elvis. The confrontation had overtones of a rebellious teenager or college student defying a parent, with Elvis seeming to forget that he was Parker's boss.

And Elvis kept taking pills. On road trips, he'd take uppers to stay awake and then downers to get to sleep. Late hours, unhealthy food, and pills that slowed his metabolism caused him to gain weight. The drugs, long hours, unsettled lifestyle, and high levels of tension frequently caused blow-ups with Elvis and his entourage. The men in the Memphis Mafia often worked with hurt feelings, or sported black eyes, from life on the road. But they were paid well.

Elvis introduced Geller to pills and the two engaged in long and trippy discussions about life and spiritualism. When the movie *Dr. Strangelove* appeared in theaters, Elvis watched it three times in one sitting, he expressed his aspirations to be a serious actor. He had grown tired of making fluffy movies, and wanted to be a dramatic actor taken seriously for his deep spiritualist philosophy.

Geller's new and overpowering presence in Elvis' life caused consternation in Col. Tom Parker, but outright jealousy with Priscilla. Now out of high school, Priscilla had developed into a beautiful twenty-year-old with a strong sexual appetite. Both her and Elvis had been convinced, since they met in Germany, that so long as they avoided penetrative vaginal sex, that they could enjoy an active sexual life before marriage and Priscilla could still be a virgin on her wedding night. But now, Elvis refused to engage with Priscilla at all, because he needed to cleanse himself spiritually. Priscilla found this new desire for purity to be upsetting, and she despised Larry Geller for the changes in Elvis.

The combination of spiritual awakening and heavy doses of all kinds of pills put Elvis on a constant trip. He saw the godhead in clouds, often dressed like a bum, and sometimes neglected his personal hygiene. Elvis turned thirty in early 1965, and there were rumors that he might get married soon. Elvis could not come down off his trips for long enough to settle down. There was a long divide between the actor and public figure he wanted to be, and the man who starred in *Harum Scarum* and gave mumbling interviews while high on pills to the few reporters who still considered him to be culturally relevant.

A television series, called *The Millionaire*, which ran on CBS from 1955 to 1960 impacted Elvis. In the show, a millionaire gave one million dollars to a random person at the start of every episode. Viewers then watched the recipient's life change over the course of an hour. This was well before the advent of reality television and the show was scripted, but Elvis wanted his money to have a positive impact on people. He started thinking about new ways he could be generous.

Although Elvis had grown up in a Mississippi shack, his parents always doted on him and he never wanted for toys or food when he was a child. Ever since the age of eighteen, Elvis had been fabulously wealthy and thought very little about money. He'd never been in a position where he had to worry about finances. This lack of concern about money, along with his newfound social conscience, started to worry more than just Col. Tom Parker. Elvis' father, his entourage members, and Priscilla all recognized that if Elvis gave away a fortune, then there wouldn't be much left over for his friends, associates, and family.

Fortunately, in 1964, Elvis' music career rebounded with a song titled "Crying in the Chapel" which made the top ten. The song also topped the British charts, showing that if the Beatles could invade the American pop scene, then Elvis could return the favor. Elvis now competed with not only the Beatles, but with the darker sounds of the British band the Rolling Stones, and the singer-songwriter Bob Dylan.

Dylan was a particular irritant because he got the kind of critical respect as an artist that Elvis desired. Dylan played acoustic guitar, sang through his nose, and the hippies considered his lyrics to be deep. The Beatles, the Rolling Stones, and Bob Dylan all had a tendency to treat fans rudely. John Lennon, in particular, employed a cruel sense of humor. On at least one occasion, Lennon stood on stage and mocked people with disabilities. Rock n' roll artists now increasingly came off as pretentious and entitled; Elvis wanted to be a man of the people.

Elvis loved cars, especially Cadillacs, and ever since he became famous, he would be occasionally gripped by the desire to give cars away. When he first started making money, he bought his mother a brand-new pink Cadillac and sometimes would give a new car away to a friend, acquaintance, or even a homeless person on the street. He frequently rewarded members of the Memphis Mafia with either stacks of cash or brand-new cars.

By some estimates, Elvis gave away about two hundred cars during his lifetime. These were not just acts of personal generosity;

they were ways that Elvis kept himself connected to everyday people. Buying gifts for his friends and associates had a way of cementing their relationships that providing salary and benefits would not have.

In 1966, while Elvis was away making a third Hawaiian movie, Col. Tom Parker made a move to put Larry Geller in his place. Parker had determined that Geller was the New Age equivalent of a Carnival showman; all that Eastern spirituality was just another con. Parker also knew that members of the Memphis Mafia were fed up with what they considered to be Geller's hippy-dippy religion.

One day, when Geller and the Memphis Mafia were all together, Col. Tom Parker showed up and put on a hypnotist act. He mesmerized one member of the entourage into acting like a monkey, and made another act like a dog. Pretty soon, Parker had turned the entire Memphis Mafia into a zoo. In case Geller didn't get the message, Parker later made another declaration. With the entourage present, Parker stated that Geller should have been a showman on the stage. From that point forward, Parker told everyone that Geller was a magician.

It was a clever tactic, on Parker's part, one that downgraded Geller from a spiritual guru to a carnival showman. Col. Tom Parker would not release his control of Elvis' career so easily. At his core, Elvis must have believed that Parker was right, because Elvis kept making movies and singing songs for the soundtracks.

# Chapter Thirteen

# Changing Times

By the end of 1965, Elvis plainly had enough of making these types of movies. He increasingly placated himself with pills and women, each of which was available to him at any time. An entourage of male friends surrounded Elvis at almost all times, but even the girlfriends of his entourage members would try to find Elvis alone. Elvis could almost never resist, and on more than one occasion had to apologize to a friend because of an affair. Elvis found that enough money could buy back the affections of just about anyone.

In her letters, Priscilla pestered Elvis about his relationships with other women. Elvis, however, took advantage of Priscilla's naivete and insisted that he remained faithful to her even as he publicly had relationships with Ann-Margret and a host of other starlets and groupies. He seemed intent to live how he wanted until Priscilla came of age, and then he would marry his pure bride and settle down.

*Harum Scarum*, like just about every other Elvis movie, raked in profits. Elvis might want to do something different, but Col. Tom Parker thought of success only in terms of money-making, not in terms of critical acclaim. If three Elvis movies and three Elvis soundtracks came out in 1965, there was no reason that three more Elvis movies and three more Elvis soundtracks could not come out in 1966.

Parker's reasoning might have kept Elvis from sinking into the tumultuous music scene at the time, which was taking a turn towards the political. In 1964, Lyndon B. Johnson easily defeated the Republican nominee, Senator Barry Goldwater. Johnson, thus, became an elected president in his own right. Johnson, a tall Texan with almost no filter on his actions or statements, pressed forward with "Great Society" legislation designed to eradicate poverty and alleviate the effects of racial discrimination. Most of the musicians other than Elvis chimed in with political opinions. Only Elvis stayed out of the fray.

Johnson also escalated the conflict in Vietnam. In 1964, the U.S. Navy reported that it had been fired upon by North Vietnamese Communists at the Gulf of Tonkin. In 1965, with an overwhelming electoral mandate behind him, Johnson escalated U.S. military involvement in Vietnam. Elvis was a healthy male at thirty years of age, but he had already served his two years during the draft and did not have to worry about being called to service again.

The last U.S. war in Korea ended before televisions were in a plurality of U.S. homes. By 1965, just about every house in the United States could claim at least one television set, many of which showed color, rather than black-and-white, images. After dinner, families regularly settled in to watch Walter Cronkite or other news anchors broadcast worldwide events. The Vietnam War, therefore, became more intensely personal to Americans than any other conflict before it.

The civil rights movement also began to show signs of black militancy. The most public example of this was in heavyweight boxing, which was arguably the most popular spectator sport at the time. The heavyweight boxing champion was considered, by most, to be the king of all athletes.

After winning gold in the 1960 Rome Olympics, light-heavyweight Cassius Clay turned professional at the age of 18. Clay quickly grew out of the light-heavyweight division, and earned a reputation as a fast-moving, and faster-talking heavyweight. As a young man, he had admired the in-the-ring antics of a professional wrestler called "Gorgeous George," who seemed to delight in provoking the crowd. Clay noted that people who bought tickets to see a wrestler or boxer be defeated paid the same amount as those who paid a ticket to see their opponent win. He began to craft a brash persona designed to draw a fan base.

Clay fought with his hands low, using his quick reflexes to avoid punches. He threw a flickering jab and stayed out of trouble with bouncing footwork. No heavyweight fighter ever used that kind of style in the ring. By 1964, Clay was undefeated and the top contender for the heavyweight title.

Yet, the heavyweight champion at the time, Charles "Sonny" Liston, seemed unbeatable. Liston grew up picking cotton in Arkansas and lived in such poverty that he never learned to read or write. When he moved to Missouri, he landed in prison where he learned to box. In the early 1950's, Sonny turned professional and worked his way up the ranks. Sonny knocked out all the top contenders, but he was so fearsome that he couldn't get a title shot.

Finally, in 1962, Sonny got his chance to fight heavyweight champion Floyd Patterson. Sonny battered Patterson to the ground twice and won the title in just over two minutes. In the rematch, Sonny knocked Patterson out in the first round again. Few people thought that Cassius Clay would last much longer than Patterson.

However, on February 25, 1964, at an arena in Miami Beach, Florida, Cassius Clay shocked the world by forcing Liston to quit in between rounds seven and eight. Cassius Clay quickly announced his allegiance to the Prophet Elijah Muhammed, Muhammed's militant and eloquent deputy Malcolm X, and the Nation of Islam. After the fight, Clay changed his name to "Cassius X." The "X" mean that Clay did not know what his real "African" name was because his ancestors had been stolen away through the slave trade. Soon after, Elijah Muhammed gave Clay a new Islamic and African named: Muhammed Ali.

Malcolm X, Elijah Muhammed, and the Nation of Islam rejected the notion of racial integration. Instead, they hoped to take over land, violently if necessary, in the West and form a separate American territory only for black people. For white Americans who were used to the integrationist approach taken by the National Association for the Advancement of Colored People, and who were used to hearing a message of nonviolent civil disobedience from Dr. Martin Luther King Jr., the message put forth by the Nation of Islam was quite a shock. Suddenly, the most recognizable athlete on the planet, the heavyweight champion, was a black desegregationist radical.

Many boxing observers thought that the victory over Liston was a fluke, or a fix, and that Liston would take the title back in a rematch. However, when Liston and Ali fought again on May 25, 1965, in the unlikely fight venue of Lewiston, Maine, Sonny went down from a light punch that most observers couldn't even see.

Liston rolled around on the ground for a little while as the referee, former heavyweight champion "Jersey" Joe Walcott, counted to ten and a little beyond. Although the fight ended under suspicious circumstances, sports fans realized that they were going to have to live with Muhammed Ali as the champion.

As champion, Ali went on a nine-fight winning streak with seven knockouts. As U.S. involvement in the Vietnam War grew more intense, it looked more and more likely that Ali would be drafted into the Army. When Ali received an official draft notice, he announced his refusal to enter the military. Ali considered the American war in Vietnam to be an expression of white supremacy, and famously said that it was not the Vietnamese communists who

Sonny (left) was 36 when he fought the then-22-year-old boxer Muhammed Ali (right).

The fight between Sonny and Ali is considered controversial, even more than 50 years later. Some call Ali's knockout punch the "Phantom Punch."

called him racial epitaphs. In 1967, Ali's title was taken from him by the courts. If he would not answer the call to be drafted, then he could not defend his title.

Ali represented a radicalism not seen before on such a public stage. When drafted into WWII, heavyweight champion Joe Louis had humbly joined the war effort. Of the two previous American heavyweight champions, Floyd Patterson had been an unassuming gentleman and a poster child of the NAACP, and Sonny Liston represented no political position at all.

Although Elvis was patriotic, white, and Christian, he recognized a kindred spirit in Muhammad Ali. Ali was as notorious, maybe more so, as Elvis had been in 1956. Both were southerners, both had attained a level of fame previously unknown in either music or sport, and both generally found it difficult to dislike other people. Muhammad Ali liked people too much to be an angry radical for long, and when public opinion swayed against the Vietnam War, Ali's refusal to go into the military was a decision that more and more Americans began to agree with.

Elvis and Donna became close friends and spent time together in-between scenes. They tended to have deep conversations about meditation and spiritual matters.

As intense as the political situation of 1966 became, making money remained Col. Tom Parker's primary ambition. The first Elvis movie of 1966 came out in March and was titled *Frankie and Johnny* with Elvis playing as a gambler named Johnny on a riverboat. Donna Douglas, better known for playing Ellie Mae in the *Beverly Hillbillies* television show, played Frankie. Together, Johnny and Frankie were boyfriend-and-girlfriend entertainers on a riverboat on the Mississippi River.

The plot featured Johnny meeting up with a gypsy fortune teller who tells him a red-headed woman will bring him luck. Johnny finds a redhead on the riverboat who does just that, but she's the boss' sort-of-girlfriend. Jealousy ensues and the boss' dimwitted stooge misinterprets the situation. The stooge saw an opportunity for revenge in a scene from Frankie and Johnny's stage show. The scene called for Frankie to shoot Johnny with blanks, but the stooge put a real bullet in the gun. The shot sends Johnny down, but he turns out to be alive because he always wore a medallion that Frankie gave him.

Audiences barely had a chance to recover from that film before the next one, *Paradise, Hawaiian Style*, was released in June of 1966. This was the last of the "Elvis in Hawaii" movies, of which there were three. The fact Elvis made the movie at all represents the resurgent force of Col. Tom Parker over Elvis' career. Parker, alarmed at his client's "religious kick," wanted Elvis to get back to making hits like 1961's Blue Hawaii.

In this picture, Elvis played Rick Richards, a newly-fired airline pilot who heads back home to Hawaii. Richards pairs up with a friend of his, Danny Kohana (played by James Shigeta), who is a Hawaiian native, and they decide to create a helicopter-tourism business. The plot of the movie featured a tension between the loose-cannon, Rick, and the straight-laced Danny. Rick's womanizing and reckless flying get him into trouble personally and professionally. Eventually, he loses his flying license.

Danny then takes out the helicopter but doesn't return. Rick faces a choice: defy his flying ban to go look for his friend, or stay grounded and obey the law? If Rick followed the rules, the movie would not have had much of an ending. As had been the case with Blue Hawaii, the lush Hawaiian scenery proved to be the real star of the movie. A helicopter turned out to be the perfect vehicle for exploring the Hawaiian islands, and the movie a perfect vehicle for having Elvis play yet another rebel with too many girlfriends and not enough money. *Paradise, Hawaiian Style* made money, but not as much as Elvis' previous movies.

Just a few months later, in October of 1966, *Spinout* was released to theaters. Elvis now played Mike McCoy, a part-time singer and part-time race car driver involved with three women at the same time. Much of the movie's tension involved McCoy trying to maintain his carefree bachelor lifestyle, while each of the three women tries to ruin it by coercing him into marriage. The three women include a spoiled heiress, a feminist sociologist using McCoy as a subject for her book about the perfect man, and the drummer in McCoy's band. The latter woman had a reputation for being a guy's girl, but that does not prevent her from scheming after her lead singer.

Meanwhile, McCoy needs to get ready for a big race, which he wins. He then develops a plan to introduce each of the three ring-hungry schemers to his male friends. Mike's hope is that, if the ladies married other men, they'd be happy and leave him alone. This plan eventually works out, and McCoy is free to live on as a happy bachelor, in love only with supped-up cars, while dating around as much he pleases.

Elvis' movies usually provided light entertainment, but with *Spinout* being released in 1966, at a time when feminism was on the rise and the civil rights movement was exploding in many American cities, Elvis' productions seemed to be a little out of touch with the times.

# Chapter Fourteen

# Dr. Nick

While Elvis filmed in Hawaii, Col. Tom Parker invited the Beatles to visit Graceland. Parker hoped that, in addition to reducing the influence of Larry Geller, he could also bring Elvis back into relevance with a younger crowd by connecting with John, Paul, George, and Ringo. Elvis had just been back home for a few days, when, on August 27, 1965, the Beatles visited. Elvis himself had little interest in the Beatles, but Parker had recognized their status as the "next big thing" back when they first came to the United States. He made a point of sending them a letter, from Elvis, wishing them luck.

Col. Parker also met with Brian Epstein, the manager and "discoverer" of the Beatles. Given that Epstein was Jewish, all-but-openly homosexual, and half Parker's age it is hard to imagine what the two had in common other than music promotions, but Parker charmed Epstein and the Beatles with gifts and promises of cross-over movie deals. Both Epstein and the Beatles were leery of visiting Elvis; they didn't need any more publicity at the time, but Parker wore them down. Parker wanted to see the press stacked deep outside of Graceland again; he wanted to use the influence of the Beatles to promote Elvis.

It's possible, even likely, that the Beatles prepared for the visit by getting stoned. Fans of both Elvis and the Beatles surrounded the gates outside of Graceland when the Beatles arrived at mid-morning, Elvis simply sat on the couch inside watching television. When the Fab Four came into the room, Elvis shook their hands, introduced Priscilla, and then played his guitar along with a jukebox. The encounter turned out to be awkward and unfulfilling. The Beatles and Elvis were all ultra-famous musicians, but really had little in common other than that.

The Beatles later spoke with contempt about their meeting

with Elvis. They considered him boring and provincial. Only John Lennon, who as a teen in Liverpool had been temporarily infatuated with Elvis, made a point to have a message of thanks sent. Elvis was largely disinterested in the Beatles and made no attempts to set up another meeting.

Towards the end of 1966, it became clear to Col. Tom Parker and the Memphis Mafia that Elvis was becoming less and less infatuated with his Eastern-mystic hairdresser and the philosophy that Geller espoused. Elvis' old interests in girls, cars, and motorcycles seemed to reemerge. In the spring of 1966, he got back into the studio to make some of the music he enjoyed. For the first time in years, he would create an album that was not made for a movie soundtrack.

This marked the first time Elvis worked with a new RCA producer named Felton Jarvis, who was close to Elvis in age and shared Elvis' enthusiasm for developing a new sound. Although Elvis had not really warmed up to the Beatles personally, he recognized the need to create a more up-tempo sound on the new album in order to keep up. Jarvis, an eccentric who owned a host of rare animals as pets, brought an enthusiasm to the project that Elvis found refreshing.

For several years, Elvis had been the hardest working actor in Hollywood and the pace seemed to have affected him. During one song, Elvis turned white and nearly passed out. Still, he seemed to enjoy the return to music and sang both gospel songs and a cover of "Stand By Me" a ballad that became a hit for Ben E. King in 1962. Elvis even recorded a song written by Bob Dylan. When the studio session ended, he had a new friend in the skinny and hyperactive Felton; they stayed in the studio and talked all night, only leaving when the employees showed up that morning to work.

The recording session was a brief respite; just weeks later, Elvis reported for work on the film Double Trouble. 1967 would mark the third year in a row where audiences could see three new movies featuring Elvis Presley. Elvis and Priscilla also finally set a wedding date for May of that year. The two had been dating for eight years and Elvis was now well into his thirties. The time seemed right for him to solidify his relationship.

Elvis' contract with Paramount Pictures, and his longstanding relationship with his producer Hall Wallis ended with the movie *Easy Come, Easy Go* which came out in March of 1967. This was Elvis' twenty-third movie. Elvis played a Navy Lieutenant named Ted Jackson, whose past career as an explosives disposal expert helps him in his new career as a deep-sea salvage diver. Luckily for the audience, Jackson also moonlights as a nightclub singer.

When Jackson finds a Spanish wreck undersea, and believes it to be full of treasure, he woos a pretty go-go girl/yoga instructor into helping him with the undersea treasure recovery. Someone else is after the treasure, however, and tries to thwart Jackson's attempts at the treasure. *Easy Come, Easy Go* represented the first financial failure for Parker's movie/soundtrack scheme. The movie actually lost money, even with Elvis singing half a dozen songs. The soundtrack LP sold only 30,000 copies, a record low for Elvis and RCA.

Just two weeks later, *Double Trouble* hit the big screen. In this film, Elvis plays Guy Lambert, a British singer who is on his way to Amsterdam. Two wealthy and beautiful women pursue Lambert. One of the women, unbeknownst to her, carries stolen diamonds in her luggage put there by a couple of bumbling jewel thieves. Inept detectives, like those featured in the Pink Panther films, also made humorous attempts at solving the case.

*Double Trouble* was the first picture that Elvis made with MGM, and he worked now with a new producer named Irwin Winkler. MGM studios barely supported the film, Winkler's first, and Elvis seemed uncomfortable in a role that had originally been written about a female European character. The studio would not spring for on-site filming, so the movie was made in nearby Culver City, California.

*Double Trouble* received better reviews than *Easy Come, Easy Go* but audience expectations had been lowered by Elvis' previous film. A few months later, the movie *Clambake* premiered with Elvis playing Scott Hayward, a rebellious heir to a fortune in oil money. After an argument with his father, the oil company CEO, Scott takes off in his Corvette. With no clear destination, Scott Hayward drives toward Florida but meets another young man, named Tom Wilson, at a gas station. Wilson doesn't have much money, but he is heading to Miami so he can work as a water-skiing instructor.

Hayward quickly bares his soul, saying how much he wished he could live as an ordinary person rather than a rich heir driving a Stingray Corvette. Tom suggests that the two switch identities and Scott Hayward accepts the premise. Now Hayward, living as Tom Wilson, is the one who goes to Miami to work as a ski instructor while Wilson goes to a hotel and lives like a rich man.

When he gets to Miami, Hayward-as-Wilson meets a beautiful young woman named Dianne Carter (played by Shelley Fabares) who is only a ski-instructor on the surface. Her real hope is to land a millionaire as a husband and she assumes that Hayward-as-Wilson intends to wed a rich widow. Of course, the two would-be gold-diggers fall in love with each other instead, even though Dianne continues to seduce a millionaire.

Meanwhile, Hayward-as-Wilson gets involved in a boat race and uses some kind of experimental outside coating to help a boat-designer win a race. Winning the boat race helps Hayward-as-Wilson finally woo Dianne, who agrees to marry him rather than the millionaire. She is pleasantly surprised to find out that her new fiancée is actually a multi-millionaire and faints with happiness upon finding out.

Elvis later declared that he considered *Clambake* to be the worst movie he ever made, but critics considered it to be standard Elvis fare. His negative attitude toward the film might have been partially due to his worsening medical conditions. *Clambake* was the first movie Elvis made after suffering a serious head and brain injury.

On a Sunday, March 5, 1967, Elvis arrived in Bel Air, Los Angeles to start filming *Clambake*. Elvis got checked out by the production team; he'd gained some weight and the wardrobe people needed to make adjustments but everything else seemed on schedule. At some point that Wednesday, while Elvis stayed at his hotel, he tangled his feet up in a cord on the bathroom floor. He tripped violently and cracked his head on the bathtub. The collision left him unconscious on the floor. No one knows how long he laid there, but he woke up on his own and started crying and cursing in pain. Priscilla, who had been sleeping, finally woke up and went to check on Elvis.

Although a sizable knot quickly formed, the fall clearly

amounted to more than just a bump on the head. Elvis apparently went to sleep and got up for filming the next day. However, when Elvis arrived at the studio he came in uncharacteristically late, and then staggered around for a while. He told his associates that he'd hit his head the night before. When doctors arrived, they found a disoriented and worried Elvis with a large lump bulging from his head.

Everyone around Elvis thought that the pills he took contributed to the fall, and the Colonel was soon called. When he arrived, Col. Tom Parker realized how hurt Elvis really was and then tore into the Memphis Mafia for failing to keep an eye on him. Doctors X-rayed Elvis but found no breaks in the skull. They diagnosed Elvis with a minor concussion and suggested rest. Col. Tom Parker blamed the influence of Larry Geller, and all but banished the hairdresser from Elvis' entourage. Parker used the occasion to take back control of Elvis' personal life and career, seeing the fall as a clear dereliction of duty from the Memphis Mafia.

Eventually, it was decided that Elvis would recover better at Graceland, so he was driven back to Memphis. On the way, he insisted on several occasions that the car pull over so that he could call local DJ's on the pay phone and put in song requests.

When he finally arrived home, Elvis claimed to see the ghost of his mother standing in her old bedroom. Elvis had likely suffered from head trauma before, the ordinary effects of a young man involved in roughhousing and the occasional brawl, but nothing so severe. Unfortunately, Elvis had met a physician named Dr. George Nichopoulos, whom everyone called "Dr. Nick," through a mutual acquaintance on February 26, 1966.

Dr. Nick was only thirty-nine at the time, but all of his hair had already turned white. His parents were from Greece and had opened a restaurant in Alabama. After graduating high school, Dr. Nick earned medical degree from Vanderbilt and joined the army, where he practiced medicine in Germany. He and Elvis got along immediately upon meeting. Dr. Nick showed no qualms about using his medical license to prescribe Elvis copious amounts of pills. Elvis, already addicted to uppers and downers, now needed painkillers for his headaches.

The head injury barely delayed filming for *Clambake*, and as soon as it was finished, Elvis had a wedding to plan. He and Priscilla, finally, were to be married on May 1, 1967.

## Chapter Fifteen

# Summer of Love

On February 19, 1963 a volume titled *The Feminine Mystique*, by an author and housewife named Betty Friedan, appeared on bookshelves. Friedan, whose personal history involved a lengthy commitment to leftist causes, had worked as a journalist prior to settling into domestic life. Her book featured "the problem that has no name," a kind of ennui, that many educated housewives settled into after marriage and children.

Few books impacted American society more deeply than *The Feminine Mystique*, and for a generation of mostly white women in the middle to upper classes, the book became an invitation into a movement either for or against the book's message. Since Friedan's book signaled a new kind of feminism, one that differed from the suffragette era that culminated, and seemed to end, with the ratification of the Nineteenth Amendment in 1920, a new era that came to be known as Second-Wave Feminism had begun.

With the civil rights movement already shaking the 1960's, Second-Wave feminism added another aspect of societal upheaval. Women demanded greater opportunities in social, legal, and professional life. Many women resented being judged primarily by their appearances, and media portrayals of women came under scrutiny. At the same time, a backlash against feminism began to form in certain conservative circles, with many men and women from more traditional, and often religious, backgrounds arguing that a woman's appropriate place was in the home.

Feminism lacked a clear consensus on how to view female sexuality. In 1953, when Hugh Hefner began publishing *Playboy* magazine, it seemed fairly clear that a magazine featuring nude or nearly nude pictures of alluring women was aimed at titillating a male audience. However, in the swinging 60's, Hefner cloaked *Playboy* in a mantle of Second-Wave feminism by declaring the women in his pages to be sexually liberated. This made some sense, after all, it had been the feminist pioneer, Margaret Sanger, who had advocated for the development of a birth-control pill. Sanger's hope had been that women could control their menstrual and fertility cycles with a pill, thereby making spontaneous, enjoyable, and pregnancy-free sex possible. When "The Pill" became available in 1960, the impact on American culture and demographics was profound and lasting.

Yet women in popular media almost always found themselves relegated to certain tasks. On the nightly news, anchormen, who were always deep-voiced and distinguished looking, led with stories about politics and science. Women, if present at all, presented human interest features. The most famous female actresses appeared as cute love interests for a macho leading man. When Sean Connery debuted as the cinematic hero James Bond, with 1962's *Dr. No*, he instituted an iconic film franchise where Bond always saved the day and a beautiful leading woman (called a "Bond Girl") was there to give him a lusty kiss, and more, as a reward for his heroics.

Yet, subtle changes could be seen in the media as well. When *The Dick Van Dyke Show* debuted in 1961, audiences who tuned into see Van Dyke play Rob Petrie, also encountered his lovely and whip-smart wife, Laura (played by Mary Tyler Moore) and the character Rose Marie (played by Sallie Rogers) who worked in a professional setting, as an equal, with other comedy writers. These women were not the stars of the show, as Lucille Ball had been in *I Love Lucy,* which debuted in 1951, but they were also not passive housewives in the way that Ball's character had been.

In 1964, the oddball sitcom, *The Addam's Family* debuted. The leading characters, a husband-and-wife team named Gomez and Morticia, not only seemed to be in a "modern" marriage (1960's style), where decision-making was shared, and there was an equal partnership, but Gomez seemed a slave to Morticia's overt sexuality and Gothic good looks.

Surrounded by the Memphis Mafia, working almost all hours on a movie set or in a music studio, and spending his leisure hours gated off from the world at Graceland, Elvis spent most of the 1960's sequestered from the major social upheavals of the time. His isolation from the outside world helps to explain why he could be so susceptible to the influences of any new person, like Larry Geller or Dr. Nick, who could break through to him. It also probably explains why Elvis' attitude toward women hardly changed throughout his life, despite the transformative social influence of feminism.

Ever since becoming famous in the 1950's, Elvis typically only came into contact with women under certain conditions: they were either groupies or actresses playing his love interests. Girls and women, seeing Elvis more as an icon than a person, tended to fawn over him. When Elvis met Sophia Loren, on the set of the movie *King Creole* in 1958, Loren was an accomplished actress a year older than Elvis. Nonetheless, she jumped into his lap and immediately started cuddling and flirting; activities captured in black and white by a photojournalist. Elvis had that effect on practically every woman he encountered.

He romanced many of these women, and more besides, but women in this era tended not to kiss and tell, so even the physical extent of his relationship with Ann-Margret, whom he claimed to have been in love with, is unknown. Generally speaking, women who dated Elvis claimed he was sweet and kind and liked to lay in bed and talk.

There was only one incident, when co-star Christina Crawford (Joan Crawford's daughter) reportedly put out one of Elvis' cigars while on the set of 1961's *Wild in the Country* with a glass of champagne, that Elvis turned violent. The sudden splash on his face shocked Elvis into grabbing Crawford by the hair and dragging her out of the room. The incident began, bystanders stated, because Elvis had been trying to watch the TV western Bonanza and Crawford wanted his attention.

Elvis and Priscilla planned to wed on May 1st of 1967; their age difference seemed less pronounced now that Elvis was thirty-two and Priscilla twenty-one. Now in his early thirties, and battling an expanding waistline, Elvis had outgrown his rebellious young man phase and was ready to settle down with his beautiful and virginal bride. Priscilla, who had spent her youth planning to marry Elvis, had little in the way of other career options, although she hoped to become an actress, which she would do after Elvis' death.

Some members of the Memphis Mafia jockeyed for position to become the best man at the wedding. Priscilla despised some of her soon-to-be husband's entourage and hoped Elvis would keep them out of the wedding, but by this time Elvis seemed to have trouble making decisions. He took more and more pills.

Photo via Flickr / Tullio Saba

Priscilla remembers her wedding day as "...private, and that's how we wanted it. We didn't want a fan club. We didn't want a circus."

No doubt, Col. Tom Parker would have rented out a sports stadium and charged top-dollar for tickets to the Presley wedding if he could have, but Elvis and Priscilla wanted to keep their nuptials quiet and intimate. Invitations went out to a select number of guests, and the guests were asked to keep quiet about the details. In late April, Elvis and Priscilla settled in at Palm Springs, California. Rumors of a marriage got out to the press, but the soon-to-be-newlyweds were a step ahead.

On Monday, May 1, two private jets flew out of Palm Springs at two o'clock in the morning. On one of the planes, owned by Frank Sinatra, sat Elvis and Priscilla. A few hours later, the planes landed in Clark County, Nevada. Elvis bought a marriage license at the courthouse at three o' clock in the morning, Nevada time, and then he and Priscilla went to the Aladdin Hotel in Las Vegas. The Aladdin was owned by one of Col. Tom Parker's friends, and Parker then directed the wedding process while Priscilla and Elvis waited. Since the wedding had to take place in a small area, Parker told the groomsmen and their wives that none of them could attend the actual ceremony. Instead, they should all plan to eat cake and take pictures afterward at the reception. The Colonel then came and called the couple out of their room and a justice from the Nevada Supreme Court married Elvis and Priscilla just before noon.

Photo via Flickr / Dan Perry

The Presley wedding cake was six tiers of yellow cake. It was extravagantly decorated with red roses and "Priscilla + Elvis" written on the 5th tier.

For the wedding and reception, Elvis was at his most charming. He and Priscilla, dressed in their finest, looked every bit like a handsome young couple in love even though they'd flown through the middle of the night. The groomsmen who'd been insulted and excluded from the ceremony at the last moment tried not to act too grumpy. Nonetheless, thousands of dollars had been poured into the reception, and nobody could stay angry for long with all the free food, champagne, and music. Vernon Presley seemed pleased to have his son married off and Priscilla's family expressed happiness at seeing the long-planned marriage finally come to fruition.

Larry Geller, who had recently been so close to Elvis that the relationship directly threatened Col. Tom Parker's control, learned about the wedding from a newspaper headline the next morning. Parker, meanwhile, was the only person, besides the judge, to attend the actual ceremony who was not a relative of either the bride or the groom. After the wedding, the newlyweds

Back in Palm Springs, the newlyweds spent their honeymoon at the "House of Tomorrow." This was their original wedding venue, before the press learned of the location. Many celebrities have since vacationed in this home.

returned to Palm Springs, then went to Graceland. They planned a larger reception for later in Memphis, but for Priscilla the three weeks between the wedding and those receptions amounted to an elongated honeymoon. She'd spent her young adulthood dreaming about, and planning to be, the wife of Elvis Presley. Now she could fully adapt to that role, and her new husband was finally home for a change. She increasingly started to resent the forces, especially the entourage around Elvis, that kept her husband away from home.

But for a few weeks, the couple enjoyed each other's company and some rare down time. Elvis and Priscilla, by all accounts, felt happy. As the Presley's enjoyed a little time away from the life of celebrity, the summer of 1967 turned into the definitive season for a tumultuous decade. With the draft causing upheaval, the civil rights movement peaking, a presidential election season beginning, and a feminist movement awakening, the United States entered the Summer of Love.

By 1967, an anti-war and generally anti-establishment movement, made up mostly of young people called hippies, became a cultural staple. Although their numbers were never large, and much of the movement radiated from college campuses, the hippie became an archetype. Male hippies wore their hair long, listened to rock n' roll, opposed the "system" and the Vietnam War. They smoked a lot of marijuana. Hippie women acted much in the same way and their embrace of peace led to the moniker of "flower children."

Part of the culture involved social gatherings devoted to peace, social justice, or just human interaction. If people could take their cars to a drive-in to see a movie with others, then why not a "love-in" or a "Human Be-In." The latter was the name for a gathering that took place at Golden Gate Park in San Francisco, California in mid-January of 1967. Timothy Leary, a middle-aged psychologist who advocated for the use of psychedelic drugs, advised the crowd to "turn on, tune in, drop out" and this became the mantra for the hippie movement in the summer of 1967.

By the summer, hippie culture controlled the Haight-Ashbury section of San Francisco. The hippies established free clinics there for medical care. Drugs flowed freely, and many of the hippies passed around both joints and copies of Jack Kerouac's free spirited 1957 novel On the Road. Many practiced "free love," a concept that was foreign, and sometimes abhorrent, to middle America. When word got out that Haight-Ashbury was the place to be for the young, hip, and anti-war, about 100,000 hippies descended on the area for a month's long communal experience.

The media, and novelists like Ken Kesey (author of 1962's, anti-establishment, One Flew Over the Cuckoo's Nest) reported regularly on San Francisco's new scene. Although most of America considered the hippie movement as a phase, millions of young people across the country started to grow out their hair, and adopted the signs and language of the hippie trend. The effect on music was to be profound, with the Beatles growing out their hair and becoming suddenly serious about social justice and the anti-war movement. Others in the music industry would follow, and the entire era would be largely defined by anti-war music.

Elvis, a married man and army veteran in his thirties, seemed irrelevant and out of touch. He was however, about to remind the world that he was the real King of Rock n' Roll.

## Chapter Sixteen

---

# Lisa Marie

By the time of his marriage, Elvis had been burned out on making movies for a long time but 1968 would see the release of three more films. Just a couple of months before his nuptials, the movie Stay Away, Joe came out in March. Based on a 1953 Peter Tewksbury novel, the movie was about a Native American rodeo cowboy who used a long Cadillac to herd cattle on the reservation. Elvis, with his skin darkened, played a character called Joe Lightcloud

Lightcloud hails from the Navajo tribe and comes up with a plan to lobby the federal government for twenty cows and a bull for the purpose of showing the country that the Navajo can raise beef just as well as the whites could. Unfortunately, Joe's ranch hand mistakes the bull for a beef animal and barbecues him. Lightcloud manages to find a replacement, but the bull fails to impregnate the cows. Stuck, Lightcloud decides to put on a rodeo where the cowboys tried to stay on the back of the bucking bull. There's also something going on with Lightcloud's parents and their need for house repairs.

The movie was fun, with lots of pretty girls trying to seduce Joe, and Elvis looking his early-thirties best in a denim get up. The movie featured a dittie with the same title as the movie, and the song jumped along well with the plot. However, MGM's executives thought that the musical numbers had run their course and significantly reduced the singing and dancing in comparison to the Paramount pictures. No soundtrack accompanied the film.

Not long after Elvis got married in May, his movie Speedway, where he played a NASCAR driver named Steve Grayson came out. Released in June, this was the Elvis movie that corresponded with the Summer of Love. Again, Elvis would play a handsome bachelor in need of money. This time, however, Grayson falls into debt through no fault of his own. Unbeknownst to Grayson, his best friend and financial manager has gambled away most of Grayson's race winnings.

As Grayson watches his belongings get repossessed, he soon realizes that he can't race without a car. Making matters worse, an IRS agent is on Grayson's tail. Luckily, the agent is a young and very attractive woman named Susan Jacks (played by Nancy Sinatra). Jacks starts off looking to collect money from Grayson, but in the end, he collects her heart.

Then, in October, another Elvis musical went up on theater marquees across the country. Live a Little, Love a Little had Elvis play a newspaper photographer named Greg Nolan. Like most of the characters that Elvis played, Nolan enjoys an uncluttered life free from the responsibilities of a wife and child. Then, while on the beach, Nolan encounters a strange woman named Bernice (played by Michelle Carey). At least, Nolan thinks her name is Bernice; she uses a plethora of different names in her daily interactions with people.

When Bernice offers an invitation to stay at her house, Nolan accepts. Then, Bernice drugs Greg so heavily that he falls into a mild coma for several days. The coma causes Greg to lose his apartment, but she makes it up to him by finding him a house. Then she helps get him two jobs as a photographer, one of which involves taking pictures of nearly naked women. Greg likes his new jobs and his new house so much that he forgives Bernice for drugging him senseless and he falls in love with her.

The movie included the song "A Little Less Conversation" which came out on the B-side of a four-song soundtrack. The song was received more favorably than the movie, which received lukewarm reviews. Reliable money makers, Elvis movies thrived on the formulaic, and critics would reliably trash the films just as readily as movie-goers would hand over money to watch them.

Elvis continued to make music, but his new recordings for RCA did not sell well. Col. Tom Parker acted as a pitchman, and knew little about how to make music. By this time, the Colonel was nearing sixty and did not understand the way in which the musical tastes of young people had changed. Ever since The Mamas and the Papas released "California Dreamin'" in 1965, the sound of popular music moved away from the bass-and-ballads form of rock n' roll that Elvis had based his early career on.

In the late 1960's, rock stations featured anti-war songs by Bob Dylan, the Doors, and the Rolling Stones. The Beatles, who adjusted quickly to the new scene, even inspired a mock-up band, the Monkees, who had a hit television show and some hit songs in the 1960's just by being a parody of a rock n' roll band. Outside of his movies, Elvis seemed to fade from the public eye. Even though he lived in luxury, he was now a married man in his thirties.

After their marriage on May 1, Priscilla became pregnant immediately and her belly swelled as Elvis went back to the movie sets. At 5:01 in the afternoon, on February 1st, nine months exactly from their wedding day, Priscilla gave birth to a little girl named Lisa Marie Presley. Nearly undone with nerves during the labor, Elvis passed out cigars when he found out that both mother and child were healthy. The day that Lisa Marie was born, he declared, was the happiest day of his life.

Four days later, Elvis, Priscilla, and their baby girl left the hospital. Priscilla paid top dollar to have her hair done up, and she wore a pink miniskirt for the cameras. For almost two weeks, they were the picture of a happy family, but when Elvis made plans to go back to work, Priscilla said she wanted to come and bring Lisa Marie. Elvis did not want his daughter going onto set and that began a rift between him and his wife. When he left home this time, it was to film Live a Little, Love a Little.

While Elvis filmed that movie, Dr. Martin Luther King Jr. visited Memphis, Tennessee in mid- March and stayed at the Lorraine Motel. King spent his time advocating for better pay and working conditions for the city's African-American sanitation workers. For a long time, King had been the subject of surveillance from the Federal Bureau of Investigation (FBI). The FBI's founder, J. Edgar Hoover, considered King to be a communist and a threat to American life. The FBI showed little respect for King's legal right to privacy, or the law in general, and acted with impunity.

Aware of threats made to his life, Dr. King made several cryptic remarks during his time in Memphis. On April 3, Dr. King spoke before a large crowd at a Christian Church and delivered the memorable line "I've been to the mountaintop" and reiterated

The birth of Lisa Marie was highly anticipated and celebrated. She was lavished with love and care from the couple – and the public!

that his death might be imminent. On April 4, Dr. King went back to his hotel room where he stayed with his friends and colleagues Ralph Abernathy and Jessa Jackson. King was standing on a balcony on the second floor, talking to friends when a gunshot rend the silence. A bullet exploded in King's face, then bored into his shoulder and spinal column.

King fell but lived long enough for an ambulance to take him to St. Joseph's hospital for emergency surgery. He died on the surgery table about an hour later. When news of the assassination traveled across the country, riots broke out in major cities like Chicago, Washington D.C., and Baltimore. JFK's brother, Robert Kennedy, happened to be campaigning for the Democratic presidential nomination in Indianapolis. Kennedy delivered the news, live, to a mostly black audience and pleaded for peace. Two months later, on June 6, 1968, Robert Kennedy too, died by assassination. Two days after that, the FBI put handcuffs on a fugitive from Missouri prison named James Earl Ray as he tried to get on an airplane destined for South Africa. Ray was soon tried and convicted for the murder of Dr. King, although the extent to which Ray acted alone has still not been clarified.

To Elvis, Dr. King's death meant more than a national tragedy; it amounted to the loss of a friend. Elvis and King met in 1961. These two men, southern and personable, found commonalities and their personalities meshed well. They kept contact over the years, and Elvis not only donated money to King's civil rights charities, but also spoke up on behalf of King and his work. For King's murder to have occurred in Elvis' beloved Memphis, made the death even more tragic.

For Elvis, as for all Americans, the spring of 1968, with the assassinations of Dr. Martin Luther King Jr. and Bobby Kennedy, plus the ongoing Vietnam War, created a tumult that seemed

Photo via Flickr / Dora Britt

With his busy schedule, Elvis was not always present in Lisa Marie's life. However, when the two were together, he spoiled her with gifts, singing, and fun experiences.

impossible to control. Even with a commanding Texan like Lyndon B. Johnson as president, the country seemed to have lost direction. Like everyone else, Elvis and Priscilla found there was little they could do but work and take care of their own family.

However, Priscilla felt increasingly abandoned by Elvis. Her husband seemed suddenly uninterested in her. Elvis proclaimed that he could not feel any sexual attraction to any woman who'd had a child, and now that Priscilla was a mother he would not approach her romantically. When Priscilla tried to initiate lovemaking, Elvis would shrug her off, and by mid-afternoon he often fell into a pill-induced stupor.

Her feelings hurt, and feeling emotionally and sexually lonely, Priscilla engaged in an extramarital affair with her handsome dance instructor. By the ethics of Elvis and the Memphis Mafia, the men could stray from their wives with impunity, but the wives needed to stand by their men and stay faithful. When some of the members of his entourage told Elvis that Priscilla seemed to spend a lot time getting private dance instruction, Elvis yelled at his friends for thinking anything bad might be going on. Elvis told the Memphis Mafia to leave Priscilla alone, and apparently continued to believe his wife to be the sweet innocent fourteen-year-old he'd met all those years ago.

Col. Tom Parker continued to direct Elvis' career, and in May of 1968, Parker met with a director named Steve Binder, and a producer named Bones Howe, both from the National Broadcasting Corporation (NBC), to discuss having Elvis act and sing in a Christmas special. Ever since Elvis hit it big in the 1950's, Parker thought that family-friendly performances appealed to the widest audiences, and thus made the most money. Although Parker carefully controlled the meeting by hosting it in his lavish MGM office, both Binder and Howe developed their own visions for a show featuring Elvis.

Steve Binder was about the same age as Elvis, and had worked on the *Steve Allen Show,* and on various rock n' roll shows. Howe worked as a sound engineer and had situated himself right in the middle of the era's hippest musical acts. Together, Howe and Binder developed a reputation for pushing the envelope when they directed a television special where a white actress named Petula Clark hugged a famous black singer/actor named Harry Belafonte before the cameras.

When the Colonel pitched the idea of a Christmas special, Binder balked at first. To Binder, Elvis seemed like a relic from the 1950's. The new generation of hippies and hipsters listened to politically-charged rock n' roll, and it was hard to see the Haight-Ashbury crowd tuning in to hear Elvis sing Christmas songs. When Binder thought of Elvis Presley, he thought of a B-movie actor. Binder's associate, Bones Howe, saved the deal. Howe had produced music with Elvis before and, like just about everyone who met the singer, found Elvis to be a pleasure to work with. Howe told Binder that the project could work if Col. Tom Parker could be sidelined.

## Chapter Seventeen

# The Comeback

Binder and Howe developed a vision for how Elvis could leave the movie business and take back control of his musical career. They invited Elvis to meet directly with them at their home offices in Los Angeles, California. Elvis knew Howe, and the conversation began with some reminiscing about the good old days. Binder, by this time, had developed so much enthusiasm for an Elvis musical special that he could hardly be contained. Binder's vision included, not Christmas songs, but a musical special devoted to telling Elvis' life story through his songs. Elvis had to catch a plane to Hawaii, but he agreed to do the show despite not fully understanding the production plan he'd been presented.

After Elvis left the contiguous United States, Binder and Howe set to working on the script for their television special. They put together a production team, and, with the olonel still believing the project to be a Christmas special, placated any concerns that Parker might have had by promising that Elvis would be paid to promote his special by making a cameo appearance on another NBC program.

None of the planning involved Elvis. He enjoyed his trip to Hawaii, where he indulged his new passion for something called Kenpo Karate. A Hawaiian Kenpo instructor named Ed Parker had connected with Elvis several years before, and Elvis found that he enjoyed studying martial arts. It was while introducing Priscilla to Ed Parker, that the Presley's also met a twenty-five year old Kenpo Karate black belt named Mike Stone. Priscilla, who had just ended her short affair with her dance instructor, found Stone to be attractive. Soon enough, Mike Stone would be her private martial arts teacher and more.

Binder and Howe developed even more enthusiasm for the project when Elvis came back from Hawaii, looking lean and tan, in early June. Elvis had embraced the late-sixties fashion of growing out his sideburns and looked to be ready to introduce himself musically to a new generation. As had been the case throughout his career, and as Howe had promised Binder, Elvis Presley was easy to work with. Presley recognized how much thought the production team had put into the script, and he trusted their judgment. By refusing to micromanage the details, Elvis could focus on perfecting his own performance.

On June 5, while Elvis smoked cigars with Binder and Howe while reviewing their script, he received word about Bobby Kennedy's assassination. Kennedy had just won the Democratic primaries in California and South Dakota, and gave a short speech around midnight at a hotel in Los Angeles. After the speech, his handlers, in direct violation of the advice given by Kennedy's bodyguard, directed Kennedy through the hotel kitchen. While walking through, a twenty-four-year-old Palestinian shot Kennedy three times with a .22 pistol. Sirhan Sirhan kept firing, wounding five more people, before being tackled. Kennedy died from the gunshots a little later at a LA hospital.

News of the assassination devastated Elvis; he'd long been fascinated with the murder of JFK and the memory of Martin Luther King Jr.'s assassination in Memphis was still raw. Elvis felt so strongly about civil rights that Binder talked about finding a way to incorporate the concept in the comeback special. By mid-June Elvis and Binder completed the script. The show would be titled *Guitar Man*, after a Jerry Reed song, and would feature Elvis with his once-trademark sneer. To placate the Colonel, Elvis would end the special with a Christmas song.

For two weeks, starting on June 3rd, Elvis rehearsed in Hollywood. Problems arose when Howe tried to record a soundtrack to the special so that he could earn money from the endeavor and NBC fired him. Then the musical coordinator quit, and Howe got rehired. Elvis sort-of rehearsed during those two weeks, and on June 17 moved to Burbank, California, so he could record the special at NBC studios.

By that time, the concept for the show involved a stripped-down performance, where the stage would be designed to give Elvis intimate contact with the audience. Audiences would be able to see Elvis sing, but also see him interact with his band and friends as a way of showcasing his personality. The recording began on June 20 with the live sessions taking place a week later in front of an audience. Col. Tom Parker put himself in charge of doling out tickets, but he never did his job so on the first day of recording, Binder walked across the street to a restaurant and asked people if they wanted to see a free Elvis show. Then he put out a radio announcement; soon enough an enthusiastic crowd filled the little theater.

Quite a bit of thought went into Elvis' wardrobe, and a clinging black leather suit eventually became the outfit of choice. Black bands and silver rings adorned his wrists and fingers. Lean from dieting and the exercise he undertook on his trip to Hawaii, and with his hair as jet-black as the leather suit, Elvis looked like an anti-establishment figure for the first time since he arrived on the scene in the 1950's. Audiences who had not paid attention to Elvis for a while might have been surprised at how young Elvis looked; he'd been around for so long that it was hard to remember that he was still just in his early thirties.

Recording the show took a couple of days. Elvis soaked the leather suit through with sweat, so it had to be hand washed and dried in between the recording sessions. Elvis, as promised to Col. Parker, played "I'll Be Home for Christmas" as his last song. The special, once recorded, sat in waiting for five months. Those months proved to be politically tempestuous in the United States, as it was a presidential election year, without an incumbent, during a time when the assassinations of both Martin Luther King Jr. and RFK put American politics in a state of turmoil and trauma.

About the same time that Elvis recorded his special, the 1968 summer Olympics in Mexico City, Mexico proved to be an arena for further controversies. On October 16, a U.S. sprinter named Tommie Smith won a gold medal, and established a world record, in the two-hundred-meter race. John Carlos, also of the U.S., finished third. The two had planned to stage a protest on the winner's podium for the purpose of drawing attention to civil rights issues in the United States. They had planned to wear black gloves, drop their heads, and raise their right fists in a "black power" salute. However, Carlos forgot to bring his gloves, so he and Smith

The black leather suit Elvis wore for his 1968 comeback TV special.

split the pair they had. Carlos wore the left glove and Smith the right glove. The picture, of both athletes with a fist raised on the winner's podium, split American opinion. The Olympics were no longer just about athletes competing.

Ten days later, a nineteen-year-old heavyweight boxer named George Foreman stopped a Soviet fighter in the second round to win the gold medal. Foreman hailed from a tough neighborhood in Houston, Texas and had learned to box in a government job corps program. When Foreman won, he wanted the crowd to know he was from the United States, so he waved a small American flag in the ring. While Foreman did not intend for his display to be a counteraction to Smith and Carlos, many commentators noted the conflicted way in which black athletes viewed their country and their place in it.

In addition to the summer Olympics, American presidential political season hit its peak in the summer of 1968. Even though he occupied the presidency, LBJ had faced a serious challenge from RFK during the Democratic nomination. LBJ won the New Hampshire primary, but by a margin so low that it would be unlikely he could go on to win his party's nomination. Rather than be publicly humiliated, Johnson withdrew from the race. Despite his advocacy for civil rights and for a "Great Society" program, LBJ's support for the increasingly unpopular Vietnam War ended his presidency.

After RFK's assassination, the Democrats nominated Hubert Humphrey, a pharmacist-turned-Senator from Minnesota. The Republicans chose Eisenhower's former vice president Richard Nixon as their candidate, even though Nixon had narrowly lost the 1960 race against John F. Kennedy. A third-party campaign, waged by Alabama Governor George Wallace, sought to roll back civil rights and reinstitute segregation. Wallace's running mate, a former Air Force general named Curtis LeMay, once orchestrated the U.S. bombing effort in WWII and made a reputation as an anti-communist hawk.

With Lyndon Johnson sidelined, Bobby Kennedy killed, Wallace tearing off Democratic votes in the once-reliable south, and a nominating convention disrupted by anti-war protests, Humphrey did not have much of a chance. Nixon won in a landslide, marking one of the most impressive political comebacks in history. He had just been elected a few weeks before Elvis' special aired on December 3.

Although Elvis taped several hours-worth of his performances, editors cut the special to just fifty minutes. The special ran on a Tuesday night at 9 pm during primetime and took the top spot in that week's ratings. Even more impressive, over forty percent of homes with televisions tuned into the special. That meant the show held the top rating for the entire viewing season. Shortly thereafter, RCA released the soundtrack and it broke into the top ten, which was a surprise considering that the show mostly involved Elvis singing well-known songs.

For his part, Elvis enjoyed singing on stage so much that he informed the Colonel that he wanted to tour again and focus on music rather than movie-making. Critical reviews of the Elvis special were almost uniformly positive, and Elvis found this to be a welcome change for how the critics wrote about his movies.

Although Elvis enjoyed working with Binder, Col. Tom Parker nearly panicked at the thought of a further collaboration. Once again, Elvis paid little attention to the details of his career and this allowed Parker to sideline Binder and once again take control of managing Elvis. In early 1969, Parker set up a new recording session, this time to make a pure album without any connection to a new movie, and Elvis could satisfy his need to sing on social issues. The top song on the album, "In the Ghetto," about a poor mother and her wayward child in Chicago, became a number one hit.

Throughout the 1960's, Rolling Stone magazine had established itself as the publication for the radical youth, and this appealed to not just hippy college students but also to high school kids who aspired to be radical youths. Rolling Stone spent most of the 1960's covering the Beatles, the Rolling Stones, Bob Dylan, and other more politically attune acts while largely ignoring Elvis. Presley's musical comeback, however, could not be ignored and in July of 1969, Rolling Stone featured Elvis on the cover.

The cover image of Elvis dressed in the black leather get-up from the 1968 television special, cemented Elvis' return to the center of popular culture. In some ways, Rolling Stone's cover feature on Elvis represented an end to the 1960's radicalism and a return to the more conservative time period of the 1950's. With Nixon in the White House and Elvis on the cover of Rolling Stone, the tumult of the Vietnam era seemed to be receding.

Nixon's term as president began with a deep irony. President Kennedy, who had defeated Nixon in the 1960 election, promised to end the decade by putting a man on the moon. Nixon would now be the president to see that promise fulfilled. The National Aeronautics and Space Association (NASA) had been founded in 1958 by President Eisenhower as a way to confront the American public's fears that Sputnik represented an insurmountable lead by the Soviets in a space race.

In 1962, JFK promised that NASA would focus on a manned

mission to the moon. A series of Apollo missions followed, each with a more complicated mission, until July 16, 1969 when Neil Armstrong set foot on the moon. His prepared declaration, "That was one small step for a man, one giant leap for mankind," provided a rare moment of unity and achievement for Americans. The moon landing provided a clear and achievable goal for an American agency at a time when the war in Vietnam seemed to lack one.

And, as the 1960's ended, Col. Tom Parker envisioned a new money-making venue for his client. Elvis Presley was going to Las Vegas.

## Chapter Eighteen

# Viva Las Vegas

Even though Elvis was in a career transition, he still had movies in the queue. In early March of 1969, the movie Charro! hit the big screens. In this Western, set in the 19th century and filmed in Arizona, Elvis played the former head of an outlaw band who, after a bunch of shoot-em-up backstory, must protect a town from his former gang.

Charro! provided Elvis a chance to act in a more grown-up drama. The film contained no sing-and-dance numbers and Elvis had plenty of opportunities to emulate Marlon Brando or James Dean. In addition to being the only movie where Elvis did not sing, Charro! was also the only film to feature a bearded Elvis. The beard fit the character well, but Elvis hated it. Not only did it mar his famous good looks, but he constantly had to scratch dust out of it in the desert heat.

Although the movie made plenty of money at the box office, it was little more than a standard B-movie western. Critics complained about the plot and more than a few audience members bought tickets expecting to see a musical. Elvis had started making the movie with high hopes of a career renewal, but by the time the picture came out he had moved onto preparing for his television musical comeback. Charro! seemed like an afterthought at the time of its release.

The last Elvis movie of the 1960's, released in November of 1969, was also the last movie where Elvis acted as a character. The title was Change of Habit. In this film, a rare combination of a crime picture and a musical, Elvis played Dr. John Carpenter, a medical doctor who works at a clinic in a poor neighborhood. He works with a nurse, Michelle Gallagher (played by Mary Tyler Moore), who also happens to be a nun. Dr. Carpenter is unaware of Gallagher's vows and falls in love with her.

Mary Tyler Moore is best known for having her own show. She won seven Emmy awards and three Golden Globes.

The nuns and Carpenter fight a corrupt system to try and help a group of kids who have learning disabilities. The movie, today, is historically notable because it provided the first big-screen depiction of an autistic person. One of the girls in the hospital presents as non-verbal with erratic behavior. While Dr. Carpenter and Gallagher never actually get together, the movie ends with ambiguity. Carpenter wants her to leave her convent and be with him, but she is unsure (and singing!) as the credits roll.

Change of Habit reflected the kind of social conscience that Elvis had expressed with his song "In the Ghetto" but the movie did poorly at the box office. Audiences might have found the sudden change of pace from previous Elvis romantic musicals to be too jarring. Also, Elvis was now a married father in middle age, and it was not clear if audiences would follow him into new roles. The lack of interest in Change of Habit, indicated that they would not. The film certainly did not hurt the reputations of two of Elvis' co-stars, Ed Asner and Mary Tyler Moore, as they went on to star in a hit sitcom called *The Mary Tyler Moore Show*.

The December 1969 television special brought Elvis back to the center of popular culture, which also mean that critics noticed Elvis again. The public loved the comeback, but some newspaper writers complained that Elvis could not sing well,  sweat too heavily on stage, didn't enunciate his lyrics, and played music that was out of touch with the times. None of the criticisms affected Elvis' ascent as a commodity, however, and Col. Tom Parker intended to develop another business model for Elvis. The movie-and-soundtrack scheme had played out. It was time for a new gig.

Col. Parker met with Alex Shoofey, a vice-president over the newly built International Hotel in Las Vegas, Nevada. The hotel reached thirty stories in height, included more than 2,500 rooms and a showroom that held 2,000 people. The hotel housed a casino and was slated to open to the public in July of 1969. The hotel owner, Kirk Kerkorian, had never graduated from junior high but had learned how to fly planes as a fighter pilot during the Second World War. After WWII, Kerkorian used his flight experience to found Transamerica airlines and used the profits from that venture to get into the casino business. The International was to be Kerkorian's crowning achievement, and he wanted to go as big as possible on its opening. There was no one bigger than Elvis Presley, and both Kerkorian and Col. Parker were eager to get Elvis scheduled as a hotel performer.

Col. Parker proposed that Kerkorian pay half a million dollars for four weeks' worth of shows. That would include one show per night and two on Saturday and Sunday. Monday would be Elvis' day off. Kerkorian agreed to the money, but wanted two shows a night and Elvis would have to be there on the hotel's opening night. In the past, only Frank Sinatra

Elvis was busy in 1970 as he performed many Las Vegas shows. His iconic look that most fans associate with him began to emerge. He wore large collars and lots of bling and eventually transitioned to wearing his famous bedazzled white suit.

could command that kind of money for shows in Vegas and Parker thought the deal to be a sound one.

Some of Elvis' friends, however, thought that two shows a night might be fine for a low-key performer like Frank Sinatra, but might not be suited to a more high-energy performer like Elvis. The pace might run Presley down. Col. Parker, as always, seemed unconcerned about the health of his client. He brushed off inquiries by stating that Elvis was a young man and could handle the pace.

Gambling turned out to be a passion for Col. Parker, although he might have liked the way that the casinos treated him as a high roller more than he enjoyed the actual gambling. Some people around Elvis thought that Col. Parker intended to yoke Elvis to an unsustainable performance schedule so that Parker could keep himself in gambling chips. In terms of raw drawing power, nobody outdid the King. Elvis would be attracting four thousand people a night when Sinatra only pulled about two thousand, and the scale of the Vegas deal created an unprecedented spectacle. It was perfect for Elvis.

At the time of the deal, Elvis had been in a rundown recording studio in Memphis making some of the best music of his career, including "In the Ghetto." When he finished his album, he flew to Vegas to sign his new contract and then see the International Hotel and Casino. When "In the Ghetto" went number one on the pop charts, the success drew attention to his new Vegas residency. With a new hit song, his movie career behind him, and his wife and child with him, Elvis moved to Las Vegas.

Around 1970, Elvis found a karate instructor, named Master Kang Rhee, in Memphis and enjoyed practicing the martial art so much that he started to incorporate karate moves into his stage show. Nervous about the Vegas act because he was not sure if he could pull enough fans to justify the cost, Elvis assembled a band and hired a costume designer named Bill Bellew to create a distinctive outfit for Vegas. The two had worked together before; Bellew made the black leather get-up that Elvis wore on the 1968 television special.

For Vegas, Bellew decided to stay away from a nostalgia piece, and instead created something that would reflect the interests that

Elvis had at the time. Elvis sometimes fell very intensely into a new interest, and in 1970 the art of karate fascinated him as much as the spiritualism of Larry Geller had just a few years before. To express this interest, Bellew built a suit that looked like a gaudy karate uniform, complete with large belts and dangling cords.

Elvis liked the outfits, and always tended to trust the judgment of the people around him when it came to career choices. Bellew's white suit became the most famous article of clothing in the history of music, as it would forever be linked with Elvis, and provided a distinctive look for Elvis impersonators.

In Vegas, Elvis continued to be easy to get along with. His band found him personable during rehearsals, and he had long been the hardest working man in show business. Col. Tom Parker, energized by the new career move, invested in a merchandising bonanza. Col. Parker paid for heavy levels of radio advertising to ensure that opening night would be a sellout, and he twisted the arm of every journalist he knew to come and cover the opening.

Finally, on July 31, 1969, Elvis took the stage wearing a black shirt, open at the neck, and a bell-bottom pants. A packed house of two-thousand fans showed that opening night. A slew of celebrities, including Fats Domino, Carol Channing, and Dick Clark, mingled with the crowd. Col. Parker had even talked Kerkorian into flying a group of journalists in to cover the opening.

Despite having rehearsed the show thoroughly, Elvis nearly suffered a panic attack before going on stage. The pressures to perform well before such an assembly, and to be the superstar draw Col. Parker had promised, wore on Elvis. At his heart, he was a performer who did not want to let the audience down, and he would sweat and fidget before a show.

An opening band was followed by a comic, and then Elvis appeared without any special announcement and played a stripped-down cover of the Carl Perkins hit "Blue Suede Shoes." The crowd loved it and, with this start in the right direction, Elvis sailed through the rest of the show and his enthusiasm spilled over to the crowd. Even the hard-bitten journalists were charmed by his connection with the audience. Most significantly of all, the performance impressed Col. Tom Parker. With tears in his eyes, the Colonel met Elvis backstage and caught his client in a bear hug. For just a few moments, Elvis seemed to be more than just a commodity.

Soon, Elvis started wearing his white karate get-up on stage. This turned out to be appropriate, one night, when Ed Parker showed up with three guests to see Elvis play the afternoon show. Parker, an American founder of Kenpo karate who had trained Elvis in Hawaii and subsequently opened some schools in Los Angeles, got special treatment during and after the show by promising to talk to Elvis about some specialized moves. During the show, Elvis incorporated some karate punches, kicks, and blocks into the performance, and then asked Ed Parker to stand up and be recognized by the crowd.

After the show, Elvis was his accommodating and good-natured self, listening to Parker's karate instructions and making Parker's guests feel welcomed. The show became a much talked-about legend in Parker's Kenpo karate schools. Parker, who trained Hollywood stunt men and choreographed martial arts movies, would later write a book about his friendship with Elvis.

For the next several weeks, until August 28th, Elvis put on two shows a day on every day but Monday. He sold out every weekend show and kept the house at near-full capacity during the week. Once seen as a scourge to god-fearing society, Elvis was now considered so mild that he sang dinner theater in front of families with children. Occasionally, the lifestyle and the pills made Elvis forget himself, and he'd unleash a few curse words on stage. Col. Parker, who was living it up at the gambling tables, chastised Elvis for this until the singer stopped.

The shows made good business sense, with Kerkorian making back about triple what he'd paid Elvis just on ticket sales alone. Of course, many of the fans who came to the International to see Elvis stayed and gambled at the hotel casino, thus increasing revenue even further. Elvis turned out to be the biggest draw that Vegas had ever seen, bringing in record crowds and revenue. After he finished, the next show up at the International involved Nancy Sinatra. Elvis hung around and saw the show, then hung out with Nancy's father, Frank. Elvis had just outearned the "Chairman of the Board" and, for once, Frank Sinatra was the second biggest thing on the Vegas strip.

## Chapter Nineteen

# **Elvis and Nixon**

Elvis followed up his Vegas trip with a country album titled *From Elvis in Memphis*. The lead song on that album, "Suspicious Minds," became not just a number one hit but one of Elvis' most-played and best-remembered songs. "Suspicious Minds" fit perfectly with Elvis' soaring vocals, and the sometimes-overwrought instrumentals featured a perfect bridge from the 1960's to the 1970's. The song itself worried some of Elvis' people, as they thought it might not hit a modern audience and the song's fadeout made it difficult to sing live, but it became not just a hit but one Elvis' best-loved songs.

Once Elvis finished his stint in Vegas he had, for the first time since he got married, nothing much to do. His expenses were high, of course, but his recent efforts put him in the black for the foreseeable future. The International's management team felt so grateful to Elvis that they granted him a significant bonus: a free trip for ten people to Hawaii. As it turned out, Elvis and Priscilla did not desire to see Hawaii again and instead decided to tour Europe.

The Colonel, showing the power he still held over Elvis, nixed the European trip because he felt that Elvis needed to sing there before he visited there, otherwise the fans of his music might get upset. For Col. Tom Parker to cancel a trip that two grown people had received as a gift shows that Elvis still considered Parker to be his manager. Parker then arranged for the Presley family and their entourage to visit the Bahamas. As soon as Elvis, Priscilla, and their friends and family arrived, a hurricane hit. They stayed just a week or so and then came home.

Elvis flew to Vegas and gambled, pretty girls at his side, at the International. When not performing, boredom overtook him. He popped pills and continued to express to Priscilla that he could not be sexually attracted to a woman who had given birth to a child. The two stopped communicating, and Priscilla grew increasingly bitter about the way that Elvis took trips without her and about the side girls that he seemed to keep everywhere.

Priscilla had Lisa Marie to take care of, but Elvis' new wife was also a young woman without a clear career path other than wife and mother. To find personal meaning, she threw herself into hobbies and interests. At one time, she studied dance, then cooking, and in the early 1970's, she came to share Elvis' passion with karate. In this, Elvis and Priscilla could be seen as in step with their times.

After WWII, servicemen who returned from the South Pacific told tales about Asian forms of fighting that did not involve weapons. American television watchers may first have encountered karate on the TV Western Wanted: Dead or Alive featuring a young Steve McQueen. A 1960 episode titled "Black Belt" featured an Asian martial artist who cleans out a saloon brawl with his bare hands. A character with some knowledge of the subject, patiently explains that some Asian martial artists developed a fearsome karate chop that could cut down trees.

McQueen himself became enamored with martial arts, and in the 1970's trained with America's first Asian acting sensation, Bruce Lee, who made a slew of martial arts action movies in the early 1970's. Priscilla developed a fascination with martial arts and began training diligently. At some point, this training brought her back into contact with Ed Parker's student, Mike Stone, and the two started an affair. Lisa Marie, still just a toddler, seemed to be aware of who Stone was but had been trained not to tattle on her mother.

Ed Parker and other martial arts experts recognized how important it was for a celebrity of Elvis' stature to promote martial arts and Parker spoke glowingly of Elvis. For his part, Elvis took more and more pills, and started to carry a pistol. He expressed that he felt he could defend himself with his karate training against anyone who was closer than six feet but carried the gun in case he was threatened by someone at a farther distance.

It might have been the case that Elvis suffered from paranoia, but the Manson Murders in August of 1969, where the actress Sharon Tate among others, were slaughtered at the behest of cult leader Charles Manson indicated that celebrities might really not be safe. The psychologically deranged Charles Manson believed that the Beatles sent him hidden messages in the song "Helter Skelter."

Col. Parker, meanwhile, settled into the life of a bad professional gambler. He lost, by some estimates, about a million dollars a year starting in 1969. The casinos left his tab open, and Parker liked the treatment he received playing games of chance. Col. Parker did not care for poker or black jack, where he might develop a skill and at least minimize his losses. He liked to roll big on the games of chance where skill did not matter and the house would, over time, always win. He was, therefore, the perfect client from the casino's perspective. Rumor had it that Col. Parker, deep in gambling debts, needed Elvis to perform in order to pay the casinos.

Soon enough, Col. Parker made arrangements for Elvis to perform again in Las Vegas, this time in January of 1970. At that time, Elvis still maintained a lean physique and in person he looked much like he did in his movies. Early on in the January Vegas engagement, the International Hotel received a kidnapping threat aimed at Elvis. Then Col. Tom Parker received a phone call from an individual threatening to kidnap Elvis, and then someone called in a threat on Elvis' life. The singer, this anonymous person promised, would be shot while performing on stage. This threat was coupled with a demand for money.

At some point, while ordering food, Elvis was given a peculiar menu with a picture of his face on the front. Some deranged person had scratched the picture up, then placed a picture of a gun next to Elvis' head and included a cryptic message asking Elvis to guess when the murder would occur. Elvis beefed up his security detail and stuffed a derringer pistol in his boot while performing. One night, when an excited fan shouted out a song request, Elvis went down to one knee and reached for his weapon before realizing the innocence of the situation.

No one ever found out who made the threats to Elvis, but some people thought it might be Col. Parker himself. The Colonel might have been afraid that Elvis would become too independent and hoped that fear would keep Elvis close to him. Or, Parker might have owed more money than anyone knew, and the threats might have been the mafia's way of warning Col. Tom Parker that no one was untouchable. The situation dissolved soon enough. Nonetheless, the combination of real danger, paranoia, drugs, and firearms made for an unstable situation. As Elvis took more pills, bought more guns, and studied more karate, he was no longer interested in being a pretty boy. Instead, he seemed to want to portray himself as a tough guy.

Always impressionable, Elvis watched the move Shaft, about an inner-city African-American private investigator (memorably played by Richard Roundtree) who kicked ass and always won his way with the women, Elvis started to wear dark clothing and walk with an intentional swagger. He obtained a license to carry a firearm and bought enough guns to arm a small militia. He liked the phrase "taking care of business" and had the initials "TCB" engraved on the handles of his guns.

Making matters worse for Elvis was the fact that his mega-celebrity status ensured that other people were all-too-willing to participate in his delusions. Elvis suddenly developed a fascination with law enforcement and reached out to random police officers everywhere. A police department in Denver sent Elvis a uniform, and he wore it proudly. Considering himself to be deputized, he paid to have police lights installed on the roof of one of his cars and intended to pull over speeders and other wrong-doers.

Richard Roundtree played John Shaft for five total *Shaft* movies. He is now known as the first Black action hero.

As 1970 wore on, Elvis noticeably put on weight. He took pills known as downers which slowed his metabolism, and in a drug-induced state he was less likely to watch what he ate. Now that he no longer made movies, the pressure to maintain a lean physique and chiseled facial features for the cameras was no longer a factor. Col. Parker planned for a barnstorming tour of six cities and intended for Elvis to make an impact at each stop.

For security, Parker arranged for local police officers to guard Elvis' entrance and even to line the route of Elvis' car. The Colonel believed that local people needed to feel like the president of the United States had arrived, and nothing made that statement like an armed motorcade. When four limousines and a massive police escort drove by, everyone knew that Elvis had come to town.

The scale of his shows, plus the drugs, seemed to make Elvis forget that he was just an entertainer. He became obsessed with wearing police badges and tried to get special gun-carrying privileges for both him and the Memphis Mafia. While in Beverly Hills, and really high on pills, Elvis took offense to a driver who flipped him off. In a bout of road rage, Elvis fired a twenty-two-caliber pistol at the car. His entourage considered Elvis unstable, and there were stories of him sticking a loaded forty-four magnum handgun right into the face of an entourage member.

As evidence that he had lost a sense of normalcy and proportion, in late 1970, Elvis acted as the best man in the wedding of a friend. As the wedding took place, Elvis stood to the side with five loaded weapons on his body. True to the Elvis mystique, they were gaudy pearl-handled and gold-plated guns, and he still tucked the little derringer pistol into his boot.

Not long after the wedding, Elvis, convinced that he needed to be a federal drug enforcement agent, left Graceland and somehow got to a public airport by himself without being noticed. He flew to Washington. On the trip, he crafted a letter to President Richard M. Nixon. In the text, Elvis expressed his deep concern about the United States because of the influences of drug culture and radical leftist groups like the Black Panthers (an assertive civil rights organization made up mostly of young African-Americans) and the hippies. Mostly, Elvis worried about the influence of communists. Elvis had studied their means of indoctrination, he wrote, and he knew how they brainwashed people.

Elvis concluded the letter by stating that, if he could just be made a federal drug enforcement agent, then he could help stop the spread of communism. He ended with an invitation to meet President Nixon and "...say hello." When Elvis got to Washington, he demanded to see an acquaintance of his, named John O' Grady, who worked at the Bureau of Narcotics and Dangerous Drugs (a forerunner of the Drug Enforcement Agency, or DEA, which would be created in 1973) but got turned away. He left his letter at the front gate and went back to his hotel.

Nixon soon received word that Elvis Presley had just come to the White House and wanted a meeting. The president directed his staff to set up the meeting and on December 21, 1970, Elvis entered the Oval Office to meet with Nixon. For the occasion, Elvis wore an open-necked blousy white shirt with a thick gold chain on his chest, purple velvet pants, a dark cape, and what looked like a

Elvis meeting Nixon at the White House.

championship boxing title belt. Sunglasses adorned his face, and he carried a cane.

It's not known how President Nixon reacted to the attire Elvis chose to wear, but Nixon was as caught up in the moment as any other fan. If Elvis wanted the badge of a Drug Enforcement Agent from the president of the United States, after giving about a day's worth of notice, then he would get one. Elvis had to interview with a member of Nixon's security team, but it was clear that Elvis was in support of the president.

After the meeting, Elvis hugged President Nixon and then made his rounds greeting the White House secretaries as he left. One of the secretaries, apparently, received a kiss. Many of Nixon's staffers described the encounter as being their favorite day in the White House. Elvis never met the FBI director, J. Edgar Hoover, directly. However, Elvis later received a letter from the FBI confirming the authority of the DEA badge.

The meeting was a testament to the power of Elvis' personality; neither man used the meeting for a photo opportunity as no press was present. The only picture taken of the two men together was kept a secret for nearly two years. Nixon's handlers remained unsure of how the public would react to the meeting. Eventually, the picture of Elvis and Nixon shaking hands would become the most requested photo in the history of the U.S. National Archives.

## Chapter Twenty

# Marriage Trouble

The 1968 comeback special and the successful show in Vegas turned Elvis into the biggest show on Earth again. Col. Parker decided to put on a show at the Houston Astrodome. The Astrodome contained 44,500 seats. Col. Parker wanted to make sure that every show sold out even as Elvis played multiple nights. The clever Parker found a way to ensure this happened. As the show approached, ticket prices plummeted all the way down to a dollar for nosebleed seats, and the show sold out for several nights.

At the beginning of the Astrodome shows, Elvis worried about how his show would carry over an arena that was designed primarily to host football games. He need not have worried; fans loved his performances so much that for the first time since the 1950's he had to escape a post-performance mob that surrounded his getaway limousine.

Not long after Houston, it was back to Vegas. Elvis' popularity seemed to rise as the country achieved more stability following the 1960's. With the Vietnam War winding down, unsuccessfully, and the murderous politics of the 1960's giving way to a more stable and boring 1970's, audiences seemed more amenable to the style of Elvis. Barefoot singer/songwriters playing protests songs on acoustic guitars were out, people now wanted to see a show.

Still, a reckoning with the sixties seemed due, and it would take place in a boxing ring. The biggest event of 1971 would not be a musical show, but a showdown for the heavyweight title. After finally being granted status as a conscientious objector to the Vietnam War, Muhammad Ali was given back his boxing license. On October 26, 1970, Muhammad Ali restarted his boxing career in Atlanta by stopping Jerry Quarry in the third round. Like Elvis, Ali had been on a public stage since he was a teenager. He was just twenty-eight-years old but seemed like an elder statesmen in the black power movement.

While Ali had been stripped of his boxing license, and therefore his title, a 1964 Olympic heavyweight gold medalist named "Smokin'" Joe Frazier had established himself as the best boxer in the world not named Muhammad Ali. Although many boxing fans considered Ali to be the champion-in-exile, Frazier won the World Boxing Association (WBA) and World Boxing Council (WBC) title belts. With his relentless head-bobbing style, and a left hook that rattled both jaws and kidneys, Frazier seemed formidable enough even for a great champion like Ali. The two seemed destined to put on the biggest sporting event in American history.

After defeating Quarry, Ali fought a top contender named Oscar Bonavena on December 7, 1970. In a sloppy fight, where both men tired badly, Ali knocked his rival out in the fifteenth and final round. It was clear that Ali's time off from boxing, where he had not always stayed fit, had taken something out of his legs. Nonetheless, plans were made to have Ali fight Frazier in Madison Square Garden for the "fight of the century."

The fight, scheduled for March 8, 1971, somehow became a reckoning with the 1960's. Muhammad Ali, the only man in the world who could rival Elvis for fame, became emblematic of the anti-war left. The three-year layoff from boxing mellowed Ali, and he reemerged in the 1970's as more of a popular public figure. Ali liked people too much to espouse, for very long, the segregationist philosophy of the Nation of Islam.

Ali's connection with the Nation of Islam had become tenuous even before Ali was stripped of his title. The Honorable Elijah Muhammad, who had given Ali his new name, became tangled in a sex scandal. Malcolm X went on pilgrimage to Mecca, and came back with slightly more conciliatory statements about race relations in the United States. In 1965, Malcolm X gave a speech in New York City and a group of assassins gunned him down.

The reasons for the murder remain unclear, but the killers seemed to have ties to the Nation of Islam itself. Most devastating to believers in black unity, the killers were all African-American. Malcolm X never reached the age of forty. The book about his life and philosophy, co-written by Alex Haley, saw publication just nine months before Malcolm X's death. *The Autobiography of*

*Malcolm X* remains a classic of book of the 1960's, and a testament to the "other side" of the civil rights movement.

In 1971, two undefeated champions in their primes (Joe Frazier, at age twenty-seven, was slightly younger than Ali) would fight for more than just the heavyweight title. The hip and leftist crowd that admired Ali's stance on Vietnam saw Ali as the people's champion. Joe Frazier, who had grown up on a hard-scrabble farm in South Carolina and learned his dangerous craft in the kill-or-be-killed gyms of Philadelphia, seemed to have no political views at all. He had not been drafted, and did not volunteer to go to Vietnam. Nonetheless, blue-collar and conservative America backed Joe Frazier to shut Ali's mouth in the ring.

The lead-up to the fight turned ugly. Ali possessed a quicker wit than Frazier, and routinely humiliated Joe with insults about Frazier's appearance. Most devastating to Frazier, Ali questioned Joe's "blackness" and commitment to civil rights. Frazier, who had fought his way out of poverty and lived in black communities his whole life, grew to hate Ali. When the two men fought on March 8, the world seemed to stop. No sporting event in American history ever captured the attention of the world like this.

It's not clear who Elvis rooted for. He certainly understood Muhammed Ali in a way that no one else could have. Yet, Elvis' politics, now that he had a Drug Enforcement Agent's badge, would seem to have made him a fan of Frazier. Elvis and Priscilla decided not to visit Madison Square Garden for the fight, and instead opted to attend a closed-circuit viewing at the Ellis Auditorium in Memphis. Elvis decked himself out in an open-neck shirt and wore a belt that looked like it could have been wrapped around the waist of a boxing champion.

The fight went fifteen brutal rounds, but Ali tired as the bout wore on. Joe Frazier just kept coming. In the last round, Frazier cocked his vaunted left hook and let it fly toward Ali's jaw. When it landed, Ali's legs buckled and he fell to his back unconscious. Ali quickly shook himself awake, and stood up before the count of ten, but he clearly lost the 15-round decision. After March 8, 1971 Joe Frazier stood as the undisputed heavyweight champion of the world. Like Elvis, Ali would come back, and the two would cross paths soon enough.

By the time of the Ali-Frazier fight, Elvis had been grinding through two shows a night in Vegas. The Vegas ventures began as a fun new way to keep his music alive and to avoid all the exhaustion involved in touring, but Col. Parker created contracts that kept Elvis trapped in the same showroom, night after night, singing the same songs and performing the same routines. Over time, the pace exhausted Elvis and probably depressed him. He'd been hoping to get away from the tiring pace of making three movies a year, but at least movie-making came with some variety.

Col. Parker, always inclined to pump his client's talent for every last cent, refused to discuss changing up the pace even though Elvis' friends expressed concerns about the performer's health. The truth was, as Priscilla noticed, Elvis could not deal with downtime. When not working, Elvis could not sit still. The intense schedule provided a consistency of sort, even if the pace was miserable.

Working nights took a toll on Elvis and the band; they stayed up late, ate unhealthy food, and then slept during the day. Always intent to give his audiences their money's worth, Elvis would don his white suit, sing his lungs out, and thrust, wiggle, and karate chop his way through a full performance until he was sweating and exhausted. Then, as the show closed, a thick cape covered in gems and rhinestones went on his back. But the pace never relented. Ordinarily, shows ran in Vegas for three to five days. Elvis played two shows a night, six days a week, for four weeks at a time. Each show ran an intense hour and fifteen minutes. He'd take drugs to wake up for the shows, and then take more to come down afterwards.

While Elvis performed, Col. Tom Parker gambled. The casino would tally Parker's debts, and Parker would schedule Elvis to cover the losses.

While in Vegas, Elvis consoled himself with women as he always had. Only now, with the unrelenting pace of Vegas, and with his pill habit overwhelming him, Elvis no longer kept his secrets very effectively. Elvis seemed to want to keep his two worlds separate; at home he could be a husband and father, but on the road he and his buddies could act as men-about-town. Elvis never allowed his entourage to bring their wives on tour, and he only worked closely with men. Just like in the movies about cowboys, army men, and athletes, women existed in their own sphere.

By 1971, Priscilla's ongoing relationship with martial arts had intensified. In America, the desire for karate competitions flourished into karate tournaments featuring new American stars like "Superfoot" Bill Wallace, Joe Lewis, Pat Johnson, and Benny "the Jet" Urquidez. The whole scene infatuated Priscilla, who would attend karate tournaments to see the quick-strike point-fighting matches, and the elaborate displays of martial arts prowess. Karate experts frequently wowed crowds with dance-like spin kicks, or by shattering boards or bricks with their feet, hands, and even foreheads. The events fascinated Elvis, but he was working and could not attend so he asked Priscilla to record the events with her movie camera.

During this period, Priscilla's relationship with karate-man Mike Stone also intensified. With Elvis gone, the two barely had to hide their affair. Priscilla, aware of Elvis' dalliances and hurt by the fact that he had not desired her sexually since she gave birth, gave Stone a fake name to use when he called or came by the Presley home in California.

Lisa Marie became a toddler and could talk, as could the maid. The maid confided to one of Elvis' friends that Stone seemed to be around a lot. Lisa Marie told her father that she'd come across Priscilla and Stone "wrestling" in a sleeping bag during a camping trip. Most telling of all, a close friend of Elvis' caught Priscilla and Stone taking a shower together, which would be an unusual martial arts lesson.

In February of 1972, while Elvis played at the Hilton in Las Vegas, the problems in the marriage erupted into a relationship-ending fight. Elvis confronted Priscilla about her affair with Mike Stone, and Priscilla let loose with five years of frustrations about her life and marriage. Elvis kept them in a bubble, he fooled around, he'd refused to be with her sexually since the birth of Lisa Marie. This last accusation prompted Elvis to initiate sex with Priscilla, but her accounts of what exactly occurred have varied over the years. She left the hotel room prepared to get a divorce.

Elvis later asked Priscilla not to go through with the separation, but she told him that their marriage really ended years before. Elvis had neglected her in favor of his career and the lifestyle of a rock n' roll star. When the divorce process began, Elvis occasionally flew into severe rages, and said he wanted Mike Stone dead. He talked of hiring a hit man to kill Stone, but nothing ever came of it. Meanwhile, Priscilla and Stone started to carry on with each other publicly and word of the affair spread.

While Elvis lived through personal turmoil, Col. Tom Parker eyed a new technology as a way to take Elvis global. Parker had heard that satellites had evolved since Sputnik went up in 1957. It was possible now to send a transmission of a performance around the globe; the ultimate carnival gimmick. Elvis kept pestering his manager to set up a European tour, but Col. Parker didn't think that a drugged-out Elvis could take the pace. Parker might also have been worried that European authorities might have learned something about his past in the Netherlands.

At that time, RCA had a new president named Rocco Laginestra, who understood the money-making potential of a show made global through satellite transmission. Col. Parker wanted Elvis to perform live in Hawaii, with the transmission going global. Elvis never really got over the death of his mother, and may never have fully recovered from the head injury after his bathroom fall. His drug habit, made worse by the trauma of the divorce with Priscilla, left Elvis vulnerable, and Col. Parker took full advantage.

The Colonel's relationship with money was always fickle. He infamously refused to pay out for music industry standards like backstage catering and never gave out free tickets to the family and friends of the band. Yet, Parker would pour money out like it was water in the Vegas casinos. Col. Parker would ring up a debt, and Elvis would sing as payment.

Col. Parker would negotiate an Elvis appearance, and demand an upfront cash payment that almost certainly went into his pocket, and then into a casino right afterward. In February of 1972, Parker created a new contract with Elvis. The contract guaranteed the Colonel one-third of Elvis' profits. Some bandmates thought that Col. Parker helped himself to all the profits on a few occasions. Elvis, who always seemed content to just have enough money to buy whatever he felt he needed, never seemed to mind. Only his father, Vernon, who had once tried so hard to keep his family fed in Depression-era poverty, expressed concern about finances.

## Chapter Twenty One

# Aloha from Hawaii

Like an aging championship boxer, Elvis got back into shape so he could perform at Madison Square Garden. A crash diet and exercise program stripped off the flab. Colonel Parker, with his outrageous new contract, now possessed more incentive than ever to get Elvis back making money on the stage. Parker knew the movie business had played out, and that Elvis would balk at making more pictures anyway, so Elvis would go to New York City for the first time in June of 1972.

New York critics tended to appreciate understated nuance more than the critics in Las Vegas did, so there was some trepidation in Elvis' camp about how his gaudy casino act would play in the Big Apple. This concern did not dissuade Elvis from decking himself out in white, rhinestone-covered suits with bell-bottom pants. He wore a "title" belt with the phrase "World Champion Entertainer" emblazoned across the buckle. The change of venue proved to be a tonic, and Elvis took the stage with new enthusiasm as he played four sold out shows in the Garden.

Oddly, neither Elvis nor Col. Tom Parker could ever be dissuaded from including a stand-up comic as the opening act for any show that Elvis played. The use of a comedian was a holdover from the 1950's variety-bit concept back when a teenaged Elvis started performing. Elvis' opening comedian always had a show that once might have played well on shows hosted by Steve Allen or Ed Sullivan. By the 1970's, audiences tended to be mystified, and sometimes enraged, when concerts started off with an old-timer sweating through moldy punchlines.

No other band used comedians as an opening act in the 1960's and 1970's, but for Elvis, the show had to start with a stand-up comic in the same way that he had to say a prayer before taking stage; it was a tradition and a good luck charm. For the comics, the experience was not always so benign. Outside of Vegas, many got viciously booed from the stage by fans who expected a contemporary musical act as the opening.

Making matters worse, Col. Parker seemed unaware of comedy beyond what he'd seen on the vaudeville stage and in Vegas nightclubs. Smaller audiences of mostly middle-aged people who went to an Elvis show for some 1950's nostalgia didn't mind the comedians, but the younger and hipper crowd reached by the more high-profile show tended to boo the comedians right off the stage. For years, a comedian named Sammy Shore opened for Elvis in Vegas but by 1972, the honor belonged to Jackie Kahane.

Kahane would become known for a one-liner, but it was not comedic. Sometime after he became the opening act in 1972, Kahane was given the job of closing Elvis' shows by coming onstage and saying, over the microphone system "Elvis has left the building. Elvis has left the building." Fans would be so worked up after an Elvis performance that they would mill around, screaming for more. Kahane not only had to open for the biggest musical act in the world with nightclub jokes; he was given the unenviable task of telling thousands of fans that their favorite act had just gone home and they should do the same.

On the night of the first performance at Madison Square Garden, the crowd viciously hooted Kahane right off the stage. When he learned about it, Elvis felt bad and made a point of going to visit his friend. Elvis said a few words of consolation. A veteran comic of the nightclub circuit, Kahane had been booed before and shrugged the incident off. The interaction highlights the way that Elvis would often go out of his way to think about other people involved in the show.

On-stage in the Garden, Elvis turned into a karate kicking, pelvic-thrusting hunk of burning love. He entered to German operatic music, and started playing like he was trying to rock the nineteen-seventies back to the nineteen-fifties. It did seem to many that, when Elvis sang, he forgot that he was heartbroken and pushing forty. Onstage he always seemed to bring the energy of a twenty-year old.

By this time, Elvis had developed two onstage staples that delighted fans. The first, discovered by accident, involved Elvis wiping sweat off his face with a white towel and then tossing the towel into the crowd. This caused many of the grown women in the audience to revert into the crazed teenagers they had once been in the 1950's, and a stack of towels were kept by the stage to keep audiences happy. The other big excitement came when a female fan was allowed on stage to receive a kiss from Elvis.

The New York shows fared better than even the Vegas dates. Col. Parker originally only planned for a three-day performance, but tickets sold so well that a fourth day got added. No one had ever sold out the Garden four days in a row before and the profits rolled in. Even more money was to be made off of the New York concerts in the future. To prevent Elvis from getting nervous, The RCA executives kept it a secret from Elvis and the band, but RCA recorded the shows for a live album. Even the usually hard-to-please New York press thought the show was a wild success, and the positive reviews helped to propel the live album sales.

One month after the New York concerts, on July 26, 1972, Elvis and Priscilla finalized their divorce terms. Priscilla received a lump sum payment, and then additional money for her personal finances and child support for Lisa Marie. The actual divorce was finalized in October of 1973. Elvis' rage over the Mike Stone affair seemed to have subsided, and he and Priscilla tried to handle the situation like adults for Lisa Marie's sake. For Elvis, the breakup stirred up a sadness he had not felt since his mother's death all those years ago. "She was one of the few girls," he said of Priscilla, "who was interested in me for me alone."

Nonetheless, thirty-seven-year-old Elvis now cavorted with a twenty-two-year-old Memphis beauty pageant queen named Linda Thompson. Upon meeting Elvis, Thompson immediately fell for his sex appeal. Thompson represented only the second long-term relationship that Elvis ever had. His first had been with Priscilla before she was of age, before the wide availability of the birth control pill, and before the sexual revolution of the 1960's. Elvis and Linda engaged in a passionate romance, and just four months into their relationship, she moved into Graceland.

Upon moving in, Linda made immediate changes to the decor of the home by ordering the addition of stained-glass windows in the entrance. Initially enamored of her new lifestyle, Linda turned her head to the pill-popping that Elvis seemed to continually engage in. Also, it quickly became clear that Elvis did not intend to take up monogamy so late in life; he wanted Linda to remain domestic and faithful while he continued his on-the-road philandering. Thompson initially tolerated, as Priscilla once had, the pills and the women.

Despite his new relationship, Elvis continued to suffer from his separation from Priscilla. He started taking harder pills, especially sedatives, that left him feeling dreary and looking drunk. Thanks to "Dr. Nick" a steady flow of prescription drugs made their way into Elvis' possession, and if he grew too tolerant of one type of pill, he would add another type. His morning cocktail of pills soon grew to include half a dozen different types of drugs.

As Elvis sank into a drug-and-depression induced haze, Col. Parker continued to negotiate terms with RCA for a satellite-broadcasted live performance from Honolulu, Hawaii. Col. Parker and RCA's executives set the show's date for January of 1973, and planned to reach almost one and a half billion viewers globally. To resolve the time zone issue; the show would be taped live and then broadcast to some locations in the United States and Europe after a delay of a few hours.

With the deal, Col. Parker pulled off two new "firsts." Not only would the satellite transmission of Elvis from Hawaii be the first truly global show, but RCA planned to release two live albums based on the show, and these would be available worldwide. With a global live performance followed by the release of two LP's, Elvis became the first superstar of Planet Earth. Back in 1953, when Sun Records released his first two-sided recording, Elvis' music only extended to a few southern states.

The plan for the show was announced in September of 1972, which gave Elvis a few months to prepare. He'd put on a considerable amount of weight and would have to lose several pounds if he was to sport a trim figure on the global stage. Probably no male performer before or after Elvis ever felt so much pressure to be thin and attractive for his audiences. Everyone who watched Elvis wanted to see him looking just as good as he had on *The Ed Sullivan Show* a decade-and-a-half before.

Between September and January, Elvis melted the flab off his body with another crash diet. His goal was to reach a weight of one-hundred-seventy-five pounds. This meant he needed to drop at least twenty pounds. To do this, he had to lay off the "downers" that slowed his metabolism. His friends and Linda Thompson hoped that a period of sobriety would put Elvis on the track to recovery, but it was not to be.

Just before taking the stage for the performance in Hawaii, Elvis ordered a shot mixed with vitamin B12 and amphetamines. When Elvis presented himself to the world, he did so on a drug high. Elvis hit the stage and sang a repertoire of his classics, but this time included a few gospel songs. Throughout it all, Elvis had always believed in the old-time religion his mother had inculcated into him back in Tupelo, Mississippi. The 1973 show featured Elvis in his iconic bejeweled white suit and cape. When the show neared its end, Elvis yanked off the cape and threw it into the crowd. Unlike the sweaty towels he usually tossed, the cape cost several thousand dollars.

The live gate for the concert went to cancer research, a fitting tribute to Elvis' lifelong devotion to philanthropy. Elvis performed in front of the Planet Earth in the same way that he used to before audiences of screaming teenage girls in high school gyms, with the full force of his talent and energy. When the show ended, Elvis left everything he had on the world's stage and then went on a drug bender.

Elvis and the band had been scheduled to visit the U.S.S. Arizona on the day after show, but Elvis had drugged himself into a stupor. He could only sit on the balcony of his hotel room, sweating and staring, as Linda Thompson explained to the band that they would not be doing any sight-seeing that day.

The show, titled *Aloha from Hawaii* drew enough international interest that it sent millions of fans to the record store. The two live albums recorded from the event went to number one, and then stayed on the Billboard Charts for the better part of a year. If it was all that Elvis had left in him, then it was a testament to how much he had.

## Chapter Twenty Two

# The People's Choice

Elvis quit acting after his thirty-first movie, but he became a star in a new kind of feature: the documentary film. In August of 1970, MGM decided to record the live performances at The International, along with backstage footage and some performances in Phoenix for a feature-length film. The film was titled Elvis - That's the Way It Is and was a high-production picture. MGM's executives chose Denis Sanders, who had won an Oscar in the Best Documentary category (for Czechoslovokia-1968, about an anti-Soviet uprising in central Europe) to direct. One of Hollywood's top cinematographers, Lucien Ballard, used eight state-of-the-art movie cameras to give audiences the full Elvis experience from multiple angles.

Elvis - That's the Way it Is came out November 11, 1970 and was met with both large audiences and favorable reviews. Documentaries were always risky prospects in the movie business, but the Elvis documentary made money. Most importantly for Elvis, the documentary proved to be a nice follow-up to his 1968 television special and a reminder to audiences that he considered himself a singer, and not an actor, once again.

In the spring of 1972, MGM commissioned another Elvis documentary that eventually came to be titled Elvis on Tour. This time, the cameras followed Elvis and his band as they rocked out in fifteen different cities. For this project, the producers were Pierre Adidge and Robert Able, who had established their industry credentials by making a documentary about Joe Cocker. One of the film editors went by the name of Martin Scorsese. Elvis on Tour received not just critical acclaim, but also official praise from Hollywood when it won a Golden Globe award.

Commercially successful in their time, the films are now historically important as they are the only recordings of Elvis and his interactions with an on-the-road audience. Onstage, he would slowly wiggle his legs or hips until the audience erupted in spasms of anticipatory cheers, then he would bounce around as if fused with nuclear energy. Somehow, Elvis in the 1970's managed to bring a Liberace-style of opulence onto the stage, strutting like only the one true King of Rock n' Roll could, while also playing up an aw-shucks innocence that reminded audiences of the young man from Memphis who had once sung to a hound dog on the *Steve Allen Show*.

The documentary films are all the more poignant, because, along with the 1973 *Aloha from Hawaii* special, they captured Elvis just before the last sad years of his decline. So too was the case with Col. Parker. Parker lived a sedentary life and ate rich foods. His weight continued to climb, and by the time his client played before an international audience in Hawaii, Parker had already been seized by three heart attacks. Morbidly obese, Parker suffered a fourth heart attack not long after the Hawaii show.

The Colonel survived, but the heart attacks put him in the hospital for days on end, and complicated his ability to care for his wife, Marie. Marie suffered from a brain ailment, most likely dementia, and declined to the point of immobility during the 1970s. It was clear that Col. Parker could not care for her, so he hired a full-time nurse at a tremendous expense.

With his wife seized by dementia, Col. Parker hired a new secretary named Loanne. Loanne's subservient attitude and her willingness to put up with Parker's unique personality, made her an ideal aide for the Colonel. At some point, the relationship developed into something more than just professional and the two became romantic.

After the show in Hawaii, Elvis declined into a depression. Elvis and Priscilla finalized their separation in October of 1973. They walked arm-in-arm out of the lawyer's office as a way of showing their ongoing amicability despite the breakup. But then Elvis fell into a pattern of excessive drug use, binge eating, and paranoid behavior. He'd starved himself of food and drugs to get into shape for the big show in Hawaii, and then went on a bender. When he returned to Vegas to play in the showroom at the Hilton, he could just barely drag himself through the show and his voice could

Los Angeles Times Photographic Collection / No alterations made

Elvis and Priscilla walking out of their divorce hearing arm-in-arm, tried to remain friends afterwards.

no longer reach the soaring heights it once had. For the first time in his career, Elvis started regularly canceling shows.

Yet, Elvis still commanded the power to attract other superstars into his orbit. One moment in February of 1973 brought together the two most defining figures of American sports and entertainment, when Muhammad Ali and Elvis finally met in Las Vegas. Ali was there to fight Joe Bugner, a European heavyweight with Australian citizenship, on Valentine's Day. Ali sometimes called himself "The Elvis of boxing" and was excited to meet the heavyweight champion of rock n' roll.

Ali and Elvis espoused different types of politics, but both also seemed to transcend traditional political divides. Both of the men were southern mama's boys who courted controversy early in their careers only to face exile, one by answering his draft notice and the other by refusing it, and then by making spectacular comebacks.

Ali had always admired Elvis. As a teenager growing up in Louisville, he listened to Elvis Presley records while the other African-American kids preferred Ray Charles. After making money in music, Elvis immediately bought his mother a new car and a house. Ali admired Elvis' devotion to his family and did the same thing for his own mother after he turned pro as a boxer. A picture of the two men, Ali in a suit and tie and Elvis in purple velvet with gold chains, shows both men looking a little puffy and past their primes.

As a gift, Ali gave Elvis a pair of boxing gloves that he autographed to read "Elvis, you are the Greatest." Elvis, in turn, gifted Ali a specially tailored robe, with the phrase "The People's Choice" spelled out in jewels. Elvis actually read the robe at the moment he gifted it to Ali and was aghast to see the phrase. It was supposed to have read "The People's Champ." Despite the mistake, Ali danced into the ring wearing the robe anyway.

By 1973, Ali could no longer dance around the ring while throwing lightning combinations the way that he had a decade earlier, but he still had enough left to defeat a rugged-but-outclassed Joe Bugner via decision. The win was Ali's ninth in a row since losing to Joe Frazier in the 1971 Fight of the Century. He kept fighting and hoping to stay relevant, so he could get another title shot.

Just a few days after the Ali-Bugner bout, Elvis had a fight of his own. As Elvis played at the Hilton, four men attacked the stage. The security detail went into action, and Elvis used the opportunity to showcase his karate training by sending one of the men backward into the crowd. Elvis then made some macho statements into the microphone, "I'm very sorry, ladies and gentlemen. I'm sorry I didn't break his goddamn neck is what I'm sorry about," before retiring backstage to find out that his foot hurt badly enough that he needed to visit a doctor.

The four men, all from Latin America, meant no harm. They apparently just wanted to meet Elvis in person and had no familiarity with performance protocol in Vegas. When this was explained to Elvis, he wouldn't believe it. As soon as he'd left the stage, Elvis had started popping pills and this caused his paranoia to swell. Elvis stated that Mike Stone, the man who's stolen Priscilla, had to be behind the stage-storming incident. Elvis told his best friend and karate partner, Red West, to go find a hitman. Mike Stone needed to die.

While Elvis raged and declined; both Col. Tom Parker and Priscilla decided they wanted new contracts. Priscilla's original divorce settlement was for a one-hundred-thousand-dollar lump-sum followed by about seventeen-hundred dollars a month for living expenses and child support. This amounted to a fortune in 1973, but still was far below what she might have gotten with a more aggressive lawyer. Now supporting Mike Stone, Priscilla decided to lawyer up and see how much more she could get from Elvis.

Col. Parker, sensing an opportunity now that Elvis both needed money and lived in a drug-induced haze, negotiated a seven-year contract with RCA. This time, however, Col. Parker wanted half the money from the deal, and that's what he got. Parker now received one-third of the earnings from any live show and one-half of earnings from recorded music. These were unheard-of percentages in a business where agents usually received fifteen percent of the money. Of course, Parker likely made even more money than was on paper since the up-front cash payments he so often insisted on never seemed to make their way into the accounting ledgers.

The truth was, Col. Parker no longer possessed his once considerable negotiating skills. It was easy enough to take advantage of Elvis, but the deal Parker cut with RCA was sub-par by industry standards. RCA typically paid out an annual income to the musicians they signed deals with. At one time, Col. Parker had insisted that Elvis always be the highest paid musical act under contract. However, the 1973 contract relegated Elvis to second-tier payments. Elvis made about half, for example of what disco star Elton John was paid.

Still, the RCA money amounted to half-a-million a year, with half of that going to Parker. If the Colonel still had a gift, it was for routing money around traditional contractual means and right into his own pocket. He would ask for "side money" to get contracts signed, and these cash-up-front deals might be why he settled for such a low annual amount for his client. Eventually, the record books would show that, of the ten and a half million dollars that RCA paid out, Col. Parker received six million.

At the same time, Priscilla's new divorce lawyers renegotiated her settlement. This time, Priscilla received almost six times her original lump sum of one-hundred thousand dollars, and about five times more than she had originally received per month for her cost of living. The new settlement also entitled Priscilla to half the worth of her former home with Elvis in California. The shock of the new settlement and Elvis' painful awareness that Mike Stone shared Priscilla's money as well as her bed, drove Elvis deeper into a depression.

More than ever, Elvis turned, repeatedly, to pills and food. The pills slowed his metabolism and the food increased his calorie count. For the Aloha in Hawaii special in January of 1973, Elvis was a slim hundred-and-seventy-five pounds. By May of 1973, Elvis weighed well-over two hundred pounds. Stoned and unwell much of the time, he canceled a show at Lake Tahoe. The incensed Colonel was forced to do the unthinkable, return money.

When it came to drugs, Elvis had the same problem that he did with his delusions about being in law enforcement; too many people were willing to indulge Elvis because of his money and fame. The Lake Tahoe incident, where Col. Parker suffered the trauma of having to give money back, apparently woke the Colonel up to the

Photo via Flickr / Dora Britt

Elvis was continually swarmed for autographs when he was in public.

seriousness of Elvis' addiction. Col. Parker knew that Dr. Nick supplied Elvis, but the quantity of pills that Elvis consumed could not come from one prescription writer alone.

The detectives reported to the Colonel that Elvis paid several different dealers, some legal physicians, some not, to supply piles of pills. Col. Parker sent forth his paid thugs to threaten these dealers, but not much changed because Elvis kept dozens of contacts for drug supply, and many were "friends of friends" which made the chain hard to track. Emotional depression, lack of physical activity, and all those drugs started to poison Elvis' organs. He suffered from bladder infections that rendered him impotent, and made it difficult to control when he urinated, so that he sometimes wet his pants. Constipation, the most routine of side effects from heavy opioid use, left him looking bloated and feeling sick much of the time.

The friends and clingers who were supposed to look out for Elvis, took almost all the money when Elvis offered it to them. All they had to do was bring him drugs.

# Chapter Twenty Three

# **Overdoses**

On June 17, 1972, five men broke into the Watergate Office building in Washington, D.C. where the Democratic National Committee headquarters were housed. Soon after arrest, the authorities discovered that the five men worked on a committee for the reelection of President Nixon. When the perpetrators went to trial, the question arose as to who the men ultimately worked for and the U.S. Senate authorized a committee to investigate the Watergate Case.

The Public Broadcasting System (PBS) covered every moment of the hearings, and in these days before cable television, this gave the hearings an unprecedented degree of political coverage. As witnesses testified, it became increasingly clear that President Nixon authorized the Watergate break-in.

As this happened, two young reporters for the Washington Post named Bob Woodward and Carl Bernstein detailed the case to a massive readership. An informer from the FBI, whose identity the reporters protected with the code name "deep throat" (decades later revealed to be an FBI agent named Mark Felt) fed the reporters information about Nixon's involvement.

By 1973, the American people increasingly began to distrust their own government. President Nixon's repeated denials regarding his involvement in the burglary, and the gangland-methods that he apparently used in trying to keep the scandal covered-up, made it clear that the highest office in the country was involved in criminal activity.

Along with the Watergate scandal, the American public largely turned against U.S. involvement in the Vietnam War. Support for the war steadily declined in the U.S. as more and more young men got called into the draft, and finally seemed to ebb away after the North Vietnamese Communists embarked on the Tet Offensive in

1968. The Tet Offensive failed in the traditional military sense, but it was a political victory in that it signaled to the American public that North Vietnam could hardly be described as nearly defeated.

After years of being promised that victory could come any time, it was now obvious that the North Vietnamese communists never intended to surrender. Equally obvious was that the United States military could not remain in Vietnam forever, especially with brutal images of the war's effects being shown on nightly news telecasts. Even normally apolitical news anchors like Walter Cronkite became vocal about the need to end the Vietnam debacle.

Upon taking office in 1969, President Nixon started to withdraw troops from Southeast Asia even as he ordered an escalation of the bombing campaign. By March of 1973, the last American soldier departed Vietnam. The American government tried to maintain some semblance of national honor with a peace treaty, but everyone could see that the American military had lost in Vietnam. The U.S. policy of indiscriminate bombing led to the deaths of likely three million Vietnamese, including U.S.-allied South Vietnamese. Fifty-eight thousand, two-hundred and twenty Americans died in the conflict. The war left Vietnam a bombed-out wreck, and many American soldiers returned home with deep physical and psychological wounds.

In the 1950's the ascent of Elvis corresponded with the rise of the United States as a postwar superpower. Now, the decline of Elvis seemed to fit with the downward direction of the country. When Elvis tried to record new music in the summer of 1973, he slurred the song so badly that the recording session had to be stopped. He tried to perform gospel music, but just ended up overpaying a band. He had drug connections everywhere and would often show up stoned for engagements.

When shows weren't canceled, journalists treated Elvis' singing with disdain and responded to his condition with alarm. High on pills and fanatical about guns and karate, Elvis became a menace to the people around him. When a groupie came to visit him in this hotel room, Elvis put a karate hold on her and accidentally broke her ankle.

The physician at the Hilton where Elvis stayed was named Elias Ghanem. Ghanem was a few years younger than Elvis and had come to the United State from Lebanon for the purpose of becoming a doctor. Ghanem liked to live the high life, hence his job in Las Vegas, and saw an opportunity to make some money supplying Elvis with drugs.

Once again, Elvis immediately took to a new friend and went overboard in showing his affection. He bought Ghanem luxury cars and Ghanem returned the affection by changing his hair, clothes, and patterns of speech to look and sound like Elvis. By October, even "Dr. Nick" could see that Elvis needed help and insisted that the singer enter the hospital. Elvis' organs were shutting down, and the weight kept piling on.

Over the course of 1973, Elvis suffered three overdoses. On more than one occasion, his heart stopped, and Dr. Nick stuck a needle full of Ritalin right into the organ in order to get it beating again. Elvis sometimes took so many pills that he lost the ability to swallow and started choking. Only the watchful members of his entourage saved his life in those instances, but no one intervened to get Elvis into a treatment center. He just kept taking drugs, but he doled out so much in money and expensive gifts that the people around him never got him the help he needed.

Elvis began the year 1974 by playing a Las Vegas engagement, but could only perform for two weeks instead of the scheduled four. By this time, Elvis wore jeweled disco-style glasses, smoked a small cigar, wore high collared shirts with a cape, and frequently carried several expensively adorned firearms. He oiled his hair into a ducktail and grew long sideburns down his cheeks.

In an attempt to take-off weight, he went on a crash diet, but the lack of food only seemed to exacerbate his lightheadedness and pills popped on an empty stomach were more potent. He wore heavy rings, and sometimes would throw performative karate punches at the heads of people he just met, pulling his fists back just inches from their faces.

While performing in Vegas, Elvis pulled out a pistol and shot into a chandelier. When he wanted drugs and could not find one of his contacts, he would throw a fit by shooting his gun in random directions. Throughout 1974, fans paid to see Elvis as a bloated and slurring sideshow, more than as a performer. He sometimes fell to the ground after shows and crawled around, too stoned to get off the floor.

If Elvis was a sideshow, the Colonel returned to his old profession and acted as the carnival barker. Col. Tom Parker kept selling tickets. He'd given up trying to cut Elvis away from the drug connections. Anyone could see that the singer, nearing forty, could not lose all the weight that he'd put on and there was no reaching him through his drug-induced haze. The only thing the Colonel could think to do was to make as much money as possible letting the public see this version of the once great King of Rock n' Roll before the curtain closed.

The Colonel could foresee that the death of Elvis would bring tremendous free publicity for merchandise featuring Elvis, and he devised a plan to take advantage. The Colonel set up a meeting with Elvis' father, Vernon, to secure the rights to Elvis' name and likeness. The resulting company, called Boxcar enterprises, featured a pair of dice each showing a six (a "boxcar" in gambling lingo) and the Colonel paid himself a salary ten times more than what Elvis received from the company annually.

While Boxcar would make money off the merchandise, the company also produced the least-remembered Elvis album. It was called *Having Fun with Elvis on Stage*. The record spliced together soundbites of Elvis joking around between songs during live performances. It was as if the Colonel, having made a fortune serving dinner, gathered up the crumbs and leftovers and sold those as a snack.

Almost all the money that the Colonel made was poured into casinos. With his wife collapsing into dementia and Elvis on the brink of death, Col. Parker kept throwing the dice and he kept losing. Vernon Presley kept an eye on the finances, and Elvis was not making enough money to sustain his entourage, band, drug habit, and Vegas lifestyle, especially not with so much money being paid out to Priscilla and siphoned off by the Colonel.

On stage at the Hilton in Vegas, Elvis increasingly voiced his frustrations during his performances. He had lost his grip on reality, and believed he could heal people by laying hands on them. Because he believed this, he visited the cancer-stricken wife of a Hilton restaurant employee. When the Hilton top-brass found out, they fired the employee for fraternizing with a celebrity guest.

When Elvis appealed to the Colonel to get the employee rehired, he found that Col. Tom Parker approved of the termination.

During a musical interlude that night on stage, Elvis went on a profanity-laced rant against the Hilton management. Col. Parker, who supported the management's decision, took the rant personally. He also recognized that his client's outburst might affect the flow of money from the Hilton. As a result, the Colonel confronted Elvis after the show and the two started shouting at each other. Elvis threatened to fire the Colonel and the Colonel offered to quit. The argument culminated with Col. Parker storming back to his hotel room where he calculated what his severance package, based on the last signed contract, would be. His bill has been lost, but it seems to have been for several million dollars.

While Elvis seemed intent on doing away with Parker, it soon became clear that he could not afford to buy out his manager's contract. Elvis employed dozens of people, and the monthly payments to Priscilla were for a fixed amount, not a percentage of income. Elvis had to settle matters with his manager and swallow the frustration along with handfuls of pills.

Increasingly, the public viewed Elvis only as a curious sideshow. Since 1970, the disco movement, which featured dance beats and a sex-and-drugs culture, started to dominate popular music. The rise of disco coincided with ongoing revelations about President Nixon's involvement in the Watergate break in. The ongoing controversy divided the United States, as it became increasingly clear that the president not only oversaw the criminal act, but actively engaged in gangster style tactics to try and cover up his involvement.

So overwhelming was the evidence that Congress could and would remove Nixon via the Constitutional process of impeachment. Not wishing to make history as the only president to be impeached, Nixon decided to resign. In November of 1973, with allegations piling up, Nixon famously declared "I am not a crook," but he would now have to admit to at least some wrongdoing.

On August 8, 1974, President Nixon gave a televised speech from the Oval Office where he announced his intention to resign the presidency. Nixon never admitted to criminality, and seemed to indicate that he was resigning because the entire Watergate scandal made working with Congress impossible, but he did acknowledge that mistakes had been made.

The next day, August 9, President Nixon turned over a letter of resignation to Secretary of State Henry Kissinger. At that moment, Nixon's vice-president, Gerald Ford, ascended to the highest office in the United States. Ford was a stolid presence for Americans. He was from Omaha, Nebraska and had played football at the University of Michigan. While Ford was an uncomplicated man, he also radiated a Midwestern sense of honesty and decency.

Yet, Nixon's resignation was not the end of the scandal. The now-former president committed crimes that could be prosecuted and the country waited for federal indictments to be issued. On September 8, 1974, just one month after Nixon resigned, Gerald Ford gave a nationally televised speech from the Oval Office where he announced that he had issued Richard Nixon a full and absolute pardon. Declaring that "...our long national nightmare is over," Ford indicated that his pardon of Nixon was intended to spare American citizens of any further trauma. The pardon, indicated Ford, would decisively end the scandal so that everyone could move on.

## Chapter Twenty Four

# Elvis: What Happened?

By 1975, the pills Elvis took caused such severe constipation that he traveled with an extensive enema kit. After an enema, he could not control his bowels and would fashion towels and sheets into an adult diaper. While drugged out, he neglected his personal hygiene and omitted offensive odors. Sometimes, when he passed out from the drugs, his entourage would drag him into the bath. They had to be careful, though, because if Elvis was only partially incapacitated, he would start throwing his weight around and cutting the air with karate-punches and chops.

Making matters worse, Vernon Presley's seventeen-year marriage to Dee Stanley ended in divorce. Elvis' relationship with his stepmother had never been warm, but it deteriorated over the years into mutual hatred. After the divorce, Dee was outside the family and could wreak havoc with malicious gossip and lies. Vernon did not look after his own health, and having seen his first wife die from addiction, he worried constantly about his only child. The divorce with Dee took a toll on Vernon's health. In January of 1975, Vernon suffered a heart attack.

News of his father's medical emergency may have triggered a panic attack in Elvis, he ended up being admitted to the same hospital as Vernon. Both the Presleys only stayed a short while, and Elvis came out of the hospital ready to resume singing in Vegas. Even in his diminished state, at forty years old, Elvis still possessed star power. He nearly landed a part in the Barbara Streisand film, A Start is Born, but the movie's producers realized Elvis could not perform effectively and negotiations broke down over money. The reality was that Elvis was no longer a big enough draw to warrant putting him in a Hollywood film.

Like Priscilla before her, Linda Thompson tired of Elvis' infidelities and began to take lovers herself. The pills likely made Elvis impotent, but strange women still came and went from his hotel room just like they had for over two decades. Still, Thompson took care of Elvis, even babied him. In so doing, she earned the respect of Vernon, who always thought that Linda Thompson really cared about his son. Unfortunately, in 1975 Linda started to realize that there was no reversing her boyfriend's drug addiction. She had doubts about the future of the relationship.

And, incredibly, the money started to run out. Col. Parker received high-dollar offers for Elvis to perform in Europe and Japan, but turned the offers down. The Colonel never liked to go out of the United States because he feared that filing for a passport would reveal his status as an illegal alien. Additionally, Elvis might get busted at customs for carrying guns and drugs. Instead, Elvis had to take out a bank loan in Memphis to cover expenses. Only recently, Elvis and the Colonel had been the highest grossing-act in Vegas history, but they now ran the bank account into the red.

Since the blow-up argument with Elvis at the Hilton in Vegas, the Colonel grew increasingly worried that Elvis would find new management. Elvis, however, seemed intent on placating the Colonel. Instead of firing Tom Parker, Elvis bought his manager a plane worth over one million dollars. Parker recognized that neither of them could afford to spend that much money on a plane, especially since Elvis owned a private aircraft himself that the Colonel could use any time.

More than anything, Elvis lived to perform on the road. When making movies, or performing at the Vegas residencies, he had to stay in one place and grind through day after day or night after night of the same dull processes and shows. He thrived on a live stage, where he could perform in new towns in front of fresh audiences. This no longer seemed possible; Elvis could not bring himself to break away from Col. Tom Parker, and the Colonel could not bring himself to schedule a European tour.

Discouraged that a new tour overseas failed to materialize, Elvis went on another pill bender. Performing in Norfolk, Virginia where his female back-up singers were both white and black, Elvis made crude and racists jokes. At the same concert, he reached out to a little blind girl who had come up to the stage. Elvis kissed a scarf and wrapped it around the girl's eyes. It was an emotional moment, but also indicates that Elvis once again believed his touch to have healing powers.

Not long after he embarrassed himself and his back-up singers with inappropriate comments, Elvis got into an argument with Dr. Nick. Elvis' doctor/pill-pusher suddenly found a conscience and decided not to write a new prescription. Elvis, elaborately decked out in firearms, pulled a pistol and started waving it around. Elvis may have been too drugged-out to know what he was doing, but he fired the gun. The discharged bullet hit a chair then bounced into Dr. Nick's chest. Thankfully, Elvis had pulled a low caliber pistol, and the chair absorbed most of the force so that the bullet only ricocheted weakly. Dr. Nick suffered a scratch, but Elvis was clearly a menace. Anybody else would have been arrested for recklessly discharging a weapon, but the incident was never reported to the police.

Once back in Vegas, Elvis took so many drugs that he could not even stand up on stage. Still, the Colonel tried one more big comeback special. The Rolling Stones were supposed to play a New Year's Eve show at the Pontiac Silverdome in Michigan, one of the biggest arenas in the country, but had to cancel days before the show. The Colonel volunteered Elvis as a replacement and sent his client up to Michigan.

Elvis drugged himself into a stupor before the show and when he waddled onto the stage in the freezing weather, the pants on his jumpsuit split down the seams. Elvis and the band he played with had little time to rehearse and were not in sync on the songs. Still, even in this condition, he was Elvis Presley and his voice sang with power. A nostalgic crowd, plied with alcohol and marijuana, watched Elvis through rose-colored glasses and cheered loudly for him as he left the stage. Even in this condition, Elvis set a record for the most money one performer ever brought in for one night.

RCA wanted Elvis to make a new album, but nobody could get him to a recording studio. Throughout his career, Elvis insisted on performing his songs with a live band just like he had at Sun Studios back in the 1950's. Recording studios quickly abandoned that form of music-making, however, and recorded individual musicians and singers separately so that the music could be spliced together later. This reduced the probability of an individual wrong-note throwing off a session and made for records that sounded better.

If Elvis was going to record new music, it was going to have to be at his house. In February of 1976, RCA's executives faced the daunting task of trying to get Elvis to record an album, with a live band, at Graceland. From the start, Elvis treated the band and the producers as welcome guests, rather than as men trying to do a job. He gave a tour of the mansion and spent hours showing off his guns, but spent very little time actually singing.

By this time, Dr. Nick, not the Colonel, became the most important person in Elvis' career. From the time Elvis woke up, until the time he went to sleep, Dr. Nick injected Elvis with everything from testosterone and methamphetamines, to natural herbs and codeine. Elvis would take uppers to get ready for a show, diet pills to get weight off, and then needed downers to counter the effects of the caffeine and methamphetamines so he could sleep. Sometimes the cocktail completely blitzed Elvis' central nervous system, leaving him with heart palpitations, slurred speech, and an unsteady gait.

By 1976, Elvis weighed seventy-pounds more than he had during the 1973 "Aloha from Hawaii" special, and was the heaviest of his life. He and the Colonel had lost almost all contact, and the original Memphis Mafia all but ceased to exist. A group of young men, mostly looking to profit from the King, surrounded Elvis now. Only Vernon seemed to really care about Elvis, as Linda Thompson left.

Still, with contracts signed, the show had to go on. Elvis wore bulky jumpsuits to hide his weight gain and would stumble onto stage and slur his way through a show. Occasionally, the old brilliance would shine through the drug-haze, but audiences mostly found Elvis' performances to be sad affairs. Some paid to see the King of Rock n' Roll in decline, but most bought tickets hoping to see Elvis at his best, only to be disappointed. Many fans thought Elvis performed while sick and didn't realize the extent of his habits.

Even Dr. Nick grew worried and started trying to wean Elvis off the hard drugs, but Elvis had too many suppliers and could always get what he wanted. Nobody had the power to put Elvis into a drug rehab clinic, and no one wanted to do without the income if Elvis went away for any length of time to get clean.

When it became clear that Elvis could not get himself clean, when it seemed certain that his drug habit would kill him, his closest friends found one more way to make money off his fame. Three men who had once acted as "bodyguards" for Elvis, until Vernon cut them from the payroll, decided to "write" a tell-all book for the mass paperback market. What hurt Elvis the most was that Red West, his best buddy since high school days, led the venture. Red's cousin Sonny West and an assistant named David Hebler pay a professional writer and reporter named Steve Dunleavy to tell their stories about Elvis.

Knowledge of the book turned Elvis into a sobbing and disoriented mess. Somewhere inside, he was still an innocent mama's boy from Tupelo, Mississippi, but so much had gone wrong. The pills, the women, the guns, and the break-up with Priscilla would all get aired out to the public. His father and Lisa Marie would be able to read about all his sins, and he knew that a public hungry for knowledge about an icon-in-decline would buy millions of copies.

Except for the professional writer, all these men had once enjoyed personal access to Elvis for years. During that time period, they had stood by and watched as Elvis popped pills and fire off his guns. They failed to intervene. Yet now that they had been fired from the entourage, they justified their book by calling it an intervention to help their friend wake up to the problems he had. None of them ever explained why this intervention could only come in the form of a tell-all book to be sold next to the tabloids.

Neither Elvis nor Col. Tom Parker could prevent the book from being published, so *Elvis: What Happened?* was scheduled for publication in the early summer of 1977.

## Chapter Twenty Five

# Elvis has left the Building

1976 was a presidential election year. Sitting President Gerald Ford had faced a challenge in the Republican primary from Ronald Reagan, a former Hollywood actor who became the governor of California. This meant that Ford would be facing Jimmy Carter, a former naval officer who became the governor of Georgia. Carter, born in 1924, had grown up on a peanut farm in Plains, Georgia during a time when the South was still segregated. He was also a southern evangelical Christian, and like a lot of southern Christians, had to reconcile his faith and worldview to a new era post the civil rights movement. Elvis felt a connection with Carter's faith, politics, and general worldview.

Ford's running mate, Bob Dole, had served with distinction in the Second World War and became a senator for Kansas. For his vice-presidential candidate, Carter chose a senator from Minnesota named Walter Mondale. Although Carter started off with a significant lead, he sometimes made missteps in his attempts to connect with younger voters. Just before the election, he agreed to conduct an interview with Playboy magazine. Although Carter made some only relatively tame admissions, his association with a publication that defined the sexual revolution seemed to defy Carter's image as a humble man of Christ.

Yet, Ford never could overcome his association with Nixon. Nor could he shed the public perception of him, spread by late-night comedians, as being a bumbling ex-jock who had trouble understanding complex issues. In November of 1976, Jimmy Carter won the presidential election with a small majority of electoral votes. He also received more than one million more votes in the popular total, an indication that the American electorate was not entirely sold on Carter as president.

During the same month of Carter's election, Linda Thompson finally left Elvis. The two had been together for about four years, ever since Priscilla walked out. While their relationship started out as passionately sexual; all those pills eventually left Elvis impotent. His belly now drooped so low that they all but hid his heavy belt buckles. Even in this state, Elvis would not go for long without attracting a woman. As soon as Thompson left, Elvis found a new girlfriend.

The new woman in his life was named Ginger Alden, a twenty-two-year-old from Memphis. Like Thompson, Alden was a beauty-pageant winner. Like Priscilla, she was young and pretty with black hair. Elvis, now in his forties, had trouble keeping up with Alden. She often spoke to him like a rebellious teen back-talking to her father. Alden was just a few years younger than Thompson, but her formative years took place during the era of women's liberation. She would not, as Priscilla had, live her life around Elvis' schedule. Nor would she, as Thompson had, resign herself to acting as a caretaker for her boyfriend.

It was never clear whether Elvis like women so much for the sex or for the company. Many of the women who spent nights with Elvis claimed that he just liked to cuddle and talk. He tended to want women around for the emotional support. Some think that he made up boasts about sexual conquests only to impress the boys-club entourage that followed him everywhere. Elvis' girlfriends, from an era where ladies did not publicly disclose such things, tend not to say much about what intimacy with Elvis consisted of. Alden may or may not have been sexually active with Elvis. It is possible that he needed a pretty young woman, and Alden looked strikingly like Priscilla, to provide him personal comfort and to keep up his public persona.

If Alden was playing the role of Elvis' girlfriend, she wanted her screen time to be minimal. Instead of hanging around Graceland, she spent time with her girlfriends and refused to chain herself to her boyfriend's schedule. While she might have refused to baby Elvis, she never refused the expensive gifts her gave her, like diamond rings, cars, and Hawaiian vacations.

The bedroom was not the only place where Elvis had trouble

Elvis, Bill Porter, and Paul Anka at the Las Vegas Hilton, 1972.

performing; on stage in Vegas he would stumble and slur his way through songs. Audiences who remembered Elvis as a trim and tan leading man from his movies, or from his shimmy-and-shake days as a cultural phenom in the fifties, barely recognized the bloated and aging man dressed in a modified karate jumpsuit who had trouble remembering lyrics. At one time, audiences crowded together to see Elvis hit high notes, now they pitied him as he seemed to hit a new low every time he took the stage. More than a few recognized that Elvis was a dying man.

By the end of 1976, the few journalists who came to see Elvis in Vegas wrote the obvious: the singer could not live much longer in such a condition. Larry Geller, Elvis' former hair stylist and spiritual advisor, had reentered Elvis' life, and privately urged the singer to take a break and get back into a healthier condition. No one seems to have suggested that Elvis enter into a rehabilitation clinic, as the concept was still fairly new and if Elvis stopped performing then no one around him would get paid. It seemed as if Elvis would abuse his body until death took him.

Elvis popped pills all day, dripped fat, slurred his speech, and stumbled when he walked, but the most obvious sign that he didn't have much longer to live was that rumors started floating around about how the Colonel finally decided to end his relationship with Elvis. The Colonel always possessed a keen business sense, and he knew that Elvis was about to stop producing money. Col. Parker never actually put his contract up for sale, but he likely started the rumor to get a sense of how much an outside investor would be willing to pay. If the price had been right, then the rumor might have become truth.

Elvis kept popping downers and eating greasy foods, so the fat kept piling on. By the spring of 1977, Elvis could only fit into one of his stage-jumpsuits and he had to wear the same one every night for almost two weeks because he would have split the pants on any of the others. When dazed on the pills, he could do almost anything. One night, perhaps thinking that his conversation with President Nixon amounted to an open invitation to call the White House, he managed to get a call through to President Jimmy Carter.

The president, surprised to be cold-called by a cultural icon, could not discern at first why Elvis had made the call. Elvis slurred his words, rambled off topic, and went silent for periods of time. Finally, Carter managed to understand what Elvis wanted. A county sheriff, apparently, had just been brought up on charges and Elvis was asking President Carter to pardon the man. Carter patiently explained that he could not issue a pardon until an actual conviction had occurred and then managed to end the call. After the disturbing interaction, Carter instructed the White House staff not to put Elvis through anymore, but this did not prevent the King of Rock n' Roll from calling the White House repeatedly over the following weeks.

Parker scheduled a tour for Elvis in the spring and summer of 1977, with Elvis performing in venues across the South and the Midwest for audiences who rarely had a chance to see big-name performers. In years prior, despite his many addictions, Elvis usually managed to keep his strangest behavior off-stage. He no longer could keep the divider up between his stage and personal life. During a Kentucky show, he told the audience he needed to use the restroom and then exited the stage, leaving his band and fans confused. After thirty minutes of awkward silence, Elvis came back on stage and started slurring through songs. His shows sometimes ended an hour or more early because he got winded from bouncing around on stage. When local doctors examined Elvis, they found him to be sick and suffering from high blood pressure and exhaustion.

By now, Elvis understood that he could not live much longer. He openly talked about death, occasionally he would mention it on stage before playing a morbid song, and he started to instruct his friends about what his funeral should look like. It was bad enough to have his decline be displayed in smaller venues throughout the country, but there was still enough demand for Elvis that he played on televised specials.

In mid-June, CBS recorded Elvis performing live in Nebraska and South Dakota on two different nights. The recording was scheduled to be broadcast in October, just after Elvis ended his summer tour. At both venues, Elvis, double-chinned and sweating, bounced around on stage in his sequined jumpsuits, and would sometimes stand at the microphone and embark on incoherent stream-of-consciousness rants. Yet, occasionally, the old Elvis arose from the depths in a clear singing voice that carried the concert to nostalgia-inducing heights.

In Vegas, Col. Parker racked up gambling debts that amounted to several million dollars, and Priscilla and her lawyers grew increasingly aggressive in demanding payments. Elvis looked like he could die at any time, so pressure grew to make money off him while he could still perform. As part of the child custody agreement, Elvis had a scheduled two weeks to spend with Lisa Marie and was pushing to finish his summer tour so that he could be with his daughter.

The Elvis summer tour

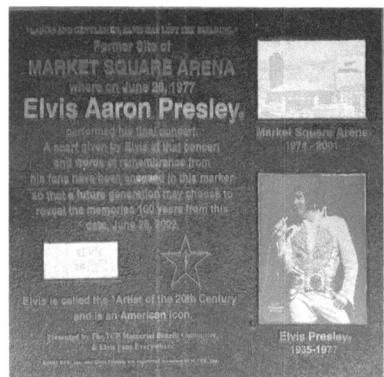

Photo via Tessa Gunderman

A plaque stands in downtown Indiapolis to commemorate Elvis' final performance in the city. Inside sits a time capsule that will be opened a century after it was compiled.

came to an end in Indianapolis, Indiana at Market Square Arena on June, 26th. When the windows opened for ticket sales, at a pricey-for-1977 fifteen dollars a pop, a line snaked around the block for about a mile. Elvis sold out Market Square Arena. Fans milled around and listened to the traditional comedian, followed by an opening musical act, then about ten o' clock at night Elvis took the stage. Overweight, but relatively sober, Elvis sang through all his classic songs, taking the audiences back to the fifties, and then hitting a crescendo with his more modern work. For just a few moments, as he stood on the stage dressed in white, he sounded like the Elvis who once shook up the country with his hip-swaying dance moves and a voice shaped by the southern blues tradition of Memphis.

When he finished, the audience erupted in applause. They stood, cheering for the King of Rock n' Roll, until a familiar voice uttered the phrase that ended every Elvis show:

"Elvis has left the building. Elvis has left the building."

In July of 1976, the long dreaded tell-all *Elvis: What Happened?* came out in the United Kingdom. Just a few weeks later, in August, the book became available in the United States. The book itself rambled on like Elvis on a pill binge, was filled with factual mistakes about Elvis' music and career and had trouble holding itself together chronologically. Nonetheless, the stories about Elvis binging on pills, engaging in reckless behavior, and then sobering up only to feel so much guilt that the process repeated itself painted a salacious picture of stardom. No figure had ever spent so much time in the public eye, and this book filled with behind-the-scenes gossip about Elvis became a bestseller.

Most readers probably understood that Elvis went through pills and women, those things could be expected of rock stars, but the reckless way in which he used firearms shocked a lot of people. According to the authors, when Elvis took too many pills he would shoot at chandeliers, and if he got mad at a television show would shoot the TV to turn it off. Certainly, there were enough public examples of Elvis' bizarre behavior to lend credibility to the accounts in the book, but the authors could never overcome their betrayal of a so-called friend. No matter how hard Red West and the other bodyguards tried to insist that the book was meant to be an intervention for Elvis, it looked to most people like a poorly written money grab.

Yet, the book defined the public's image of Elvis Presley in his final years.

## Chapter Twenty Six

# **Graceland**

August of 1977 was supposed to bring some respite for Elvis. He'd planned to spend most of the month in Graceland, relaxing with his new girlfriend and spending some rare time with Lisa Marie. Elvis' daughter had already turned nine-years old, and spent most of her time in California with Priscilla. However, the publication of *Elvis: What Happened?* robbed Elvis of peace of mind.

The tell-all book enraged Elvis so much that he shouted openly, and frequently, about bringing the authors to Graceland to murder them. The only other time Elvis ever spoke of killing someone had been when he casually talked of hiring a hit man to kill Priscilla's boyfriend, Mike Stone. Elvis likely made these threats just to blow off steam, but the people around him, recognizing that a man so heavily armed and heavily drugged might be capable of anything, thought the statements made Elvis seem unhinged.

Elvis could no longer fit into most of his rock-star outfits, so instead of going out into public in rhinestone-covered jumpsuits, he opted for designed sweatsuits. On the front of his sweatsuit jackets, proudly displayed, he always wore the DEA agent badge he'd procured from President Nixon. As a general rule, Elvis carried a couple of .45 caliber pistols as an accessory, and frequently kept a derringer in his boot and sometimes another firearm or two just in case.

To lose weight, Elvis went on another fad-diet, this time he only ate Jell-o and the lack of nutrition and calories left him feeling light-headed and tired. Years of playing night shows in Vegas distorted Elvis' sleep patterns, so that even when he went home to Graceland for a rest, as he did in August of 1977, he tended to sleep all day and stay up at night.

Such was the case on August 14, when Elvis took his girlfriend,

Ginger Alden out for a motorcycle ride. Elvis always instructed his entourage to "sleep when I sleep," so he had people to talk with as evening turned into midnight and then early morning. Early in the morning on August 15, he spoke at length with his hairdresser and spiritual guru, Larry Geller, and spent some time talking with Alden. Always a Christian believer, Elvis spent some time reading a popular book about the Shroud of Turin. The arrival of dawn was the signal for Elvis to start popping downers so he could sleep, and he took a handful just before eight in the morning.

Normally, Elvis slept from eight in the morning to four in the afternoon and Alden had adapted these hours as well. Just before bed, Elvis took off his track suit and put on a pair of silk pajamas. Alden laid down with him in the cavernous Graceland bedroom and went to sleep. At some point, Elvis got out of bed and went into the bathroom. At a little after two in the morning, Alden woke up by herself in the bed. Concerned, she pulled back the covers and walked into the bathroom, where she found the corpse of Elvis Presley.

Shocked, Alden went to the intercom system and called for help. When the bodyguards arrived, all they could do was confirm the obvious. Elvis, face down in a shaggy bathroom mat, with his pants around his ankles, dried blood caked on his nostrils, and what was left of his tongue hanging out his mouth between his clenched teeth, had been dead for long enough to turn stiff.

In the ensuing chaos, no one thought about Lisa Marie, and she stood in the hallway watching as the Graceland staff rushed in and out of her father's bedroom. For most of her life, she'd only seen her father during breaks in his career or the few weeks of the year when she was allowed to visit as the custody arrangement allowed. Her summer visit to Graceland would be the end of her childhood; she'd arrived in Memphis just in time to see her father die. Her grandfather, Vernon, was present but fell to the floor. His weak heart, already stressed by the long-ago death of his wife, the collapse of a second marriage, and years of worrying about his son, threatened to give out entirely. Vernon rose in time to instruct that Elvis be taken to the hospital.

Throughout his life, everyone seemed to cater to Elvis' delusions because he was so famous, and so it would be in this final, macabre scene. Everyone pretended Elvis was not dead. Elvis was stiff with rigor mortis and his skin had gone black from the pooled blood, yet the paramedics took his body to the hospital. A team of emergency room doctors and nurses tried for a while to revive a dead body, then gave up and declared Elvis Presley to be deceased.

Col. Tom Parker, who had stationed himself in Portland, Oregon to prepare for Elvis' next tour, got the news by phone. The Colonel ordered one of his aides to go to Graceland to be with Elvis' father, then busied himself spreading the news of Elvis' demise. There were tour dates to cancel, business to be done, new kinds of money to be made. He flew to New York to make sure he could negotiate favorable terms with RCA for all of the Elvis merchandise that would now sell because of the publicity surrounding the death of such an entertainment icon.

In shock, Lisa Marie called the one woman she had always associated with her father, a woman who'd always been kind, Linda Thompson, and told her of the death. Thompson consoled the little girl she'd seen so much of over the years, and their private conversation in grief provided just a few moments of solace before news of Elvis' death led to an international outpouring of collective sadness. The hospital staff officially pronounced Elvis to be dead, of a heart attack, about 3:30 in the afternoon on August 16, 1977. Elvis Presley lived only forty-two years.

All over the country, newspapers printed special editions with bolded headlines announcing the death of Elvis Presley. The daily news segments of the major networks led with the tragedy. For middle-aged Americans, of an era that saw the early deaths of so many leading political figures and entertainers, the loss of Elvis brought up familiar feelings of grief. Elvis had been with them since the time when James Dean died and had been the definitive figure in the adolescent years for so many. Millions of women who had fallen in love with Elvis from afar, grieved his death with personal force.

Such was the public outpouring of emotion, that the Presley family decided to have an open casket funeral at Graceland. Tens of thousands of people lined the Memphis Streets to try and get a glimpse of the deceased King of Rock n' Roll, with many hyperventilating from the heavy grief and humidity in the air.

President Jimmy Carter dispatched three-hundred National Guard troops to provide direction and security. The Presley family, gracious in their understanding that Elvis belonged to everyone, decided to allow the open casket but merely asked that no photographs be taken of Elvis' body as it laid in state.

Journalists from the gossip rag, the National Enquirer, had other ideas. They slipped eighteen grand to Billy Mann, a cousin of Elvis, to sneak a picture of the body. Mann took the money and the photo. The picture of a dead Elvis promptly ran on the cover of the next issue. The money turned out to be well-spent, as that issue of the National Enquirer sold more copies than any other in the publication's history.

After the public viewing, the actual funeral took place on August 18 with only two hundred people allowed to attend. Amongst the Hollywood elite, the funeral took on the connotations of any other exclusive event and several celebrities made time to attend, with John Wayne being the most prominent. Ann-Margret, the most famous of Elvis' past girlfriends and co-stars, was also there in addition to Burt Reynolds, who owed much of his famous look and personality to Elvis.

Over eighty-thousand people lined the streets to see the funeral process. Many of the mourners took the time to write signs expressing their love and grief. The procession ended at the Forest Hill Cemetery, where Elvis was buried next to the body of his beloved Mother, Gladys Love Presley.

Most conspicuously, Col. Tom Parker arrived looking as if he were ready to watch a baseball game or play a round of golf in Hawaii. Dressed in a baseball cap, casual slacks, and a Hawaiian shirt, Parker smoked a cigar and seemed to take the death of Elvis in stride. He had, after all, already established control of most of the profits from Elvis-themed merchandise. The Colonel understood the power of free advertising and the funeral coverage for a celebrity of this magnitude would send the grieving masses off to the store where they could express their sadness by purchasing mugs, T-shirts, and lunchboxes featuring the visage of Elvis Presley. When asked to be a pallbearer, the Colonel declined.

It took a few days for everyone around Elvis to process the shock, but then the armchair theorizing about the cause of death began.

No one believed that Elvis died at the hospital in the afternoon; he'd clearly died in the early morning hours of August 16. Some doctors believed he fell off the toilet, unconscious, and that the heavy shag-carpet cut off his air. Some people thought Elvis committed suicide via overdose, or that he'd taken a handful of the wrong pills and died from his body's reaction. Of course, many believed in the bizarre conspiracy theory that Elvis still lived, and that his death and funeral were fakes. Tabloids would continue to report "Elvis sightings" for decades.

In October of 1977, the official coroner's report revealed that a drug overdose killed Elvis Presley. He had mixed pills, probably ten different kinds, in such a way that the toxins overwhelmed his system. Just a few days later, a medical examiner contradicted these findings by saying that Elvis died of heart disease. The pills, stated Dr. Jerry Francisco, did not kill Elvis. Many began to understand the unfortunate reality that, by the time of his death, Elvis was always under the influence of pills, and this made it difficult to discern their effects on the actual cause of his death.

Eventually, it was revealed that "Dr. Nick" had prescribed Elvis with about 19,000 pills over the course of their relationship. Over that time, Elvis also established an untold number of connections to other physicians and drug dealers. In effect, Elvis slowly poisoned his organs over the course of almost two decades by overloading his system with repeated doses of uppers and downers.

Everyone but Vernon and the Colonel thought that Elvis would leave behind a fortune, but not much remained. Too much money went through the Colonel's hands and into the profits of the casinos in Las Vegas. Too much went to Dr. Nick, or any of the other pill pushers. Elvis and the Colonel were like a magic act; Elvis would conjure money out of thin air and then Col. Tom Parker made it disappear.

Someone figured that there was money, still, in the corpse of Elvis Presley. Just a few days after the funeral a graverobber tried to dig up Elvis. He was caught, but for security's sake the caskets of Elvis and his mother were removed from Forest Hill cemetery and reburied in the Meditation Garden at Graceland. Gladys Presley, who suffered the death of Elvis' twin, and loved her surviving son through the depths of her grief and the hard times of the

Depression, who died from the grief of her separation from him, finally got to be reunited with her boy. Elvis, who never recovered from his mother's death, finally found his eternal rest next to her.

# Chapter Twenty Seven

# Transitions

For many Americans, the late 1970's represented a period of decline and transition. The controversies over Vietnam left the country scarred and divided, while the Watergate scandal eroded public trust in traditional governmental institutions. Even the excitement over the 1969 moon landing quickly faded, as subsequent missions failed to generate much interest or new science. Unable to justify the continued cost and risk of the moon landings, NASA discontinued the landings in 1972, the last year of the U.S. involvement in Vietnam and the first year of the Watergate scandal.

Jimmy Carter returned morality to the White House, but high gas prices and a 1979 revolution in Iran, where Shiite Islamic revolutionaries seized fifty Americans as hostages, dissolved the public trust in Carter's judgment and policies. Despite being a southern evangelical himself, Carter could not direct a Christian movement that trended to conservative politics. In 1980, Carter lost the presidency to a former actor and governor of California, Ronald Reagan. Elvis had once promoted polio vaccines for Truman, gotten a DEA badge from Nixon, and cold-called President Carter. Ronald Reagan would be the first president since Truman to not have any contact with Elvis.

Muhammad Ali, the only other icon of the time who could claim to be as famous as Elvis, stepped into the ring just a few weeks after Elvis died. In 1974, Ali had regained his title under suspicious circumstances by knocking out the undefeated champion George Foreman in Kinshasa Zaire in a bout dubbed "The Rumble in the Jungle." Now well into his thirties, and battered by three ring-wars apiece against Joe Frazier and Kenny Norton, Ali stepped into the ring with a murderous puncher named Earnie Shavers.

In the second round, Shavers cracked Ali with a right hand

that sent the champion stagger-stepping across the ring, but Ali gradually recovered as the fight went on. In the fifteenth round, with the outcome of the fight still in the balance, Ali's feet regained their wings and he danced around the ring with the energy of his youth, cutting the air with punches, and popping Shavers with sharp combinations. It was to be the last moment of greatness for the champion. He won a decision, but his next two fights against Leon Spinks, where Ali lost and regained his title, would reveal Ali to be a ghostly shell of his younger self, with Parkinson's disease and the accumulation of punches having the same effect on Ali that the pills once had on Elvis.

After defeating Spinks in a September 1978 rematch, Ali retired for two years. He decided to make a comeback in 1980 to fight undefeated heavyweight champion Larry Holmes. Holmes had once been Ali's chief sparring partner, but time had clearly changed both men. The fight turned into a sad affair, with Ali barely throwing any punches while Holmes landed at will. Finally, Ali's trainer, Angelo Dundee, saved the aged and beaten fighter by stopping the fight between rounds.

Although Ali lived in a time of deep racial strife, and for a time repeated the "white devil" rhetoric of the Nation of Islam, he never had a bad word to say about Elvis. In 1975, Elvis came to Ali's training camp in Pennsylvania and the two men got along like old friends. Saddened by the death of his favorite rock musician, Ali visited Graceland in 1978 to express his condolences to Vernon. In 1985, Ali visited Graceland again and spoke about how much Elvis meant to him. Ali declared Elvis Presley to be "the greatest of all time" which was high praise for a man who only ever used that title for himself. Elvis and Ali both danced in places where nobody ever had before, on-stage and in a boxing ring, and shocked the world by doing it.

No band defined the 1960's like the Beatles; their music even penetrated across the Iron Curtain, with innovative young Soviets making bootleg records of the Fab Five by using discarded X-Rays. However, by 1970, personality conflicts and creative differences frayed the music group. Brian Epstein, their manager and the architect of Beatlemania, died of a drug overdose at the age of thirty-three. For years, Epstein handled the strain of managing four titanic egos while hiding his homosexuality. His father's death tipped Epstein into a final pill-popping bender.

Just a few months after Epstein's death, John Lennon met and fell in love with a Japanese artist named Yoko Ono. Ono's controlling behavior and abrasive personality wore on George, Ringo, and Paul, as did Lennon's increasing dependence on heroin. By 1970, McCartney spoke openly to the press about not wanting to be in the band anymore, and a year later formed the music-group Wings. With Paul's wife, Linda, on the keyboards Wings produced several hits including the memorable "Band on the Run."

In 1971, John Lennon released a solo album that included the classic song "Imagine," which might have been the last and greatest of the hippie ballads. With that song, he established an identity separate from the Fab Four and he seemed to cultivate an image for himself as an English rock star with the soul of an Eastern mystic. The Beatles formally disbanded, in the truest sense of the word, in 1974.

On the evening of December 8, 1980, a deranged young man named Mark David Chapman visited New York City, where he asked John Lennon to sign an album cover. Lennon did, and then went off to a recording session. When Lennon returned home with Yoko Ono that night, Chapman stood waiting near the doorway of the Lennon residence. Upon seeing Lennon, Chapman raised a .38 special revolved and fired five shots at Lennon, four of the bullets pierced Lennon in the back and he died on the scene.

Chapman's grievance with Lennon had something to do with Lennon's flippant comment, fourteen years earlier, about the Beatles being bigger than Jesus. A pudgy man who imbibed a steady diet of Twinkie snack cakes, Chapman considered himself an outsider like Holden Caulfield in the J.D. Salinger classic The Catcher in the Rye. Indeed, Chapman carried a copy of that novel with him on the day that he murdered Lennon and sat calmly reading it as the police arrived. The death of John Lennon, forty years of age, reminded rock fans that fame held many dangers other than too much money and too many pills.

In December of 1977, just a few months after Elvis died, the movie *Saturday Night Fever* was released. The movie starred a young John Travolta, who had already won over a female audience by playing a dimwitted high schooler on the hit sitcom "Welcome Back, Kotter" in his first major acting role. As Tony Mareno, Travolta cut up the disco dance floors while wearing a white suit that looked like a toned-down version of Elvis' Las Vegas costume. Travolta's flamboyant dance moves, complete with hip thrusts and pointing fingers, did not look much different than the karate moves that Elvis cut the air with on Vegas stages during his final years.

In many ways, *Saturday Night Fever* followed in the movie/soundtrack format first created by Elvis and the Colonel. The Australian disco/pop group, the Bee Gees, performed the soundtracks top song "Stayin' Alive" and both the movie and the song defined the late seventies as the disco generation. *Saturday Night Fever* was a musical without being called one and an Elvis movie without Elvis.

As disco dominated culture and the radio air waves, a new cultural phenomenon began to spread from the dance clubs of the Bronx and Brooklyn. In about 1973, disc jockeys started scratching records for rhythm, and the most skilled could use multiple turntables to create a hip-hop cadence that young dancers found irresistible. From this, a new musical genre known as rap formed. In 1980, a rap group called the Sugar Hill Gang released a song titled "Rapper's Delight" and the musical movement grew from there. Rap was as different from the love ballads that Elvis first sang at Sun Studios as two kinds of music can be, and it became a defining feature of black musical culture.

In August of 1981, Music Television (MTV) debuted as a cable network with, appropriately enough, a song and video by the Buggles titled "Video Killed the Radio Star." Soon enough, MTV turned into the dominant feature of American youth. The music video, a short piece of performance art pioneered by Elvis in Jailhouse Rock back in 1955, became a primary way for musical artists to introduce themselves to fans.

In 1982, Michael Jackson reached an Elvis-level of fame with the release of his album *Thriller*. In homage to Elvis, known forever as the King of Rock n' Roll, the press dubbed Jackson to be the "King of Pop" (pop being shorthand for popular music). The "Thriller" music video, featuring the creepy-voiced B-movie horror staple

Vincent Price, included an elaborate dance sequence featuring zombies. When Jackson danced with the undead, he paid an unwitting homage to the young Elvis Presley who once did the same on-screen with singing prisoners.

Jackson's affiliation with Pepsi also echoed the Elvis/Tom Parker model for turning fame into merchandising. In the mid-1980's, Michael Jackson signed a lucrative deal with the soda company as Pepsi tried to connect with a younger demographic. In a memorable 1984 incident, on-set pyrotechnics set Jackson's hair on fire. As was the case with Elvis, Jackson soon suffered from the peculiar seclusion brought on by extreme fame. His costumes became increasingly elaborate and bizarre, with him wearing only one glittering glove. Also, like Elvis, Jackson soon became addicted to pills.

About the same time that Jackson made his mark on the popular music landscape, the artist known as Prince (a year later, he would be formerly known, as he changed his name to a symbol) released the album *Purple Rain*. In true Elvis fashion, Prince starred in a semi-biographical movie, also titled *Purple Rain*, that featured the hit songs of his album as the soundtrack. Prince was a uniquely talented songwriter, and as such his music is remembered long after the movie has been forgotten, but his career path seemed almost predetermined by Elvis. Prince, too, would become addicted to pills and died as a result.

Of all the entertainers who followed Elvis in the 1980's, Madonna comes to the closest to emulating Elvis. Like Elvis, Madonna introduced herself to her fans with overtly sexual dance moves. While it was never true that the 1950's were a more innocent time, it was true that audiences in the 1950's tended to relegate sexy forms of entertainment to "red light" districts. They expected their television shows to be relatively clean. MTV brought sexy entertainments into the mainstream.

At the 1984 Video Music Awards (VMAs), Madonna rolled around suggestively, wearing a lacy wedding dress, while singing her hit "Like a Virgin." Audiences had not been so scandalized since Elvis swiveled his hips at the Louisiana Hayride in the 1950's. Like Elvis, Madonna also starred in a series of films where she also sang on the soundtrack, such as 1985's Desperately Seeking Susan.

Unlike Elvis, Madonna would eventually gain respect as a "real actor" as she co-starred in the 1990 summer blockbuster Dick Tracy and had a solid speaking role in the 1992 baseball classic *A League of Their Own*. It is telling, however, that when director Penny Marshall cast Madonna in the latter movie, the actress Debra Winger refused to be in the film and accused Marshall of making an "Elvis movie."

Cher was another singer known by a single name. In 1988, she won an Oscar for her role in the hit movie *Moonstruck*. Few people would have associated her win with Elvis Presley, but when Cher won the Academy Award she became the first singer-turned-actress to win the support of her peers. Elvis, who once pined for the respect of movie critics while hoping for the chance to act in serious dramatic roles, certainly would have appreciated Cher's achievement. In her accomplished life, Cher also won an Emmy, Grammy, and three Golden Globe Awards. In interviews, she admits to one great regret. She had a chance to date Elvis in the 1960's and turned it down.

## Chapter Twenty Eight

# The Show Must Go On

Vernon Presley lived for almost two years after the death of his son, but a heart attack sent him to the hospital in the summer of 1979. He died in the hospital on June 26, having endured the loss of his wife, his only son, and the breakup of a second marriage. Vernon, everyone agreed, deserved to be called a good ol' boy. His ex-wife, Davada "Dee" Stanley-Presley hardly waited for Vernon's body to go cold before she tried to make a cash-grab with two "tell-all" books where most of what she had to tell was a bunch of lies.

Dee hated Elvis from the beginning of her relationship with Vernon, and Elvis returned the sentiment. She publicly vented her hatred for Elvis on several occasions and never felt accepted into the Presley inner-circle despite her marriage to Vernon. After 1977's publication of *Elvis: What Happened?*, it was clear that a market existed for books about Elvis' extreme behaviors. Dee decided to take advantage of that market and published two books about Elvis.

In those books, Dee asserted that Elvis was bisexual. She also stated that his marriage to Priscilla had been forced by the families. The death of her stepson, she stated, occurred by suicide because Elvis could not live with the knowledge of a bone cancer diagnosis. Her most disgusting accusation, and the one most guaranteed to make tabloid headlines and sell books, involved Elvis engaging in an incestuous relationship with his mother, Gladys.

The books made money even though the claims had no basis in facts. No male has ever come forward to say he had a sexual relationship with Elvis. Priscilla never claimed to have been forced to marry Elvis. None of Elvis' doctors ever came forward to share that the singer suffered from bone cancer, and the official autopsy report said nothing about either bone cancer or suicide. The accusation of incest, made well after Elvis and his parents were dead and unable to sue for libel, says more about Dee than it does about Elvis or Gladys. Dee Stanley Presley largely disappeared from public view after the publication of her tabloid-books and died in 2013.

Not long after her divorce with Elvis was finalized, Priscilla broke up with Mike Stone because he'd authored a salacious article titled "How I Stole Elvis Presley's Wife" for a gossip rag. Priscilla was just thirty-two years old and single when her ex-husband died. She still radiated with beauty and talent. In many ways, her life and career were just beginning. When Elvis died, Vernon took control of the Presley estate. He always liked Priscilla and sympathized with her position, so he made Priscilla the executor in the event of his death. When Vernon died in 1979, Priscilla took control of the Presley assets and she quickly found out that the taxes and cost of upkeep for Graceland would soon drain her resources.

Quickly, Priscilla realized that Graceland could only survive as a tourist attraction and she hired a firm to turn the private residence into a public museum dedicated to Elvis' music, movies, and life. In June of 1982, Graceland opened to the public. Priscilla's decision turned out to be a brilliant business move as the investment started turning a profit just four weeks later, and Graceland remains a popular destination that draws tourists from around the world to Memphis.

Subsequently, Priscilla created Elvis Presley Enterprises, thus outmaneuvering Col. Tom Parker, and in so doing created a company that came to be valued at more than one-hundred million dollars. When Lisa Marie turned twenty-one, she took control of the company. Priscilla also created a line of fragrances and other beauty products that she sold on the Home Shopping Network through the 1980's and 1990's.

Most people remember Priscilla for her acting roles in the 1980's and 1990's. Having accumulated wealth through her businesses, she could afford to be careful about the roles she chose, and she turned down an offer to be one of the butt-kicking angels on Charlie's Angels. Later, she would also turned down a role as the Bond Girl in 1985's A View to a Kill. Priscilla eventually started acting on television in 1980 and had roles on well-known programs like The Fall Guy. Most famously, she played Jenna Wade on the mega-hit primetime soap opera *Dallas*. After five years, Priscilla quit the show.

Deciding to try comedy, she co-starred with Leslie Nielsen in 1988's sleeper hit *The Naked Gun: From the Files of Police Squad!*. The movie was a popular and critical hit that spawned two sequels featuring the Nielsen-Presley co-stars. Comedy suited Priscilla, and she also starred in a 1990 vehicle for the flash-in-the-pan comedian Andrew Dice Clay titled *The Adventures of Ford Fairlane*. Throughout the 1990's, Priscilla stayed relevant by working on a variety of hit television shows, including the prime-time hit Melrose Place. After a long hiatus from acting, Priscilla returned by playing the Wicked Queen in *Snow White and the Seven Dwarfs* at a London theatre.

Priscilla never married again, but she was romantically linked to a number of men including Robert Kardashian. After Robert and Priscilla broke up, Robert married Kris Houghton, who became Kris Kardashian. Kris and Robert had four children together before divorcing in 1991. Shortly thereafter, Kris married the famous Olympic decathlete, Bruce Jenner. Robert died of cancer in 2003. In 2007, Kris, Bruce and the children all became celebrities when the reality show *Keeping Up with the Kardashians* aired on the E! Entertainment network, with Kris's daughter Kim becoming the defining female celebrity of the era.

Prior to marrying Kris, Bruce Jenner had been married to Elvis' ex-girlfriend, Linda Thompson. After leaving Elvis, Thompson found fame on the hit CBS country-music and comedy variety show *Hee Haw*, where she played a beautiful hillbilly woman as a comic foil. She and Bruce Jenner married in 1981, had two sons, and then divorced in 1986 after Bruce revealed to Linda that he liked to dress in women's clothes.

In 1991, Thompson married the record producer David Foster. In 2005, Linda Thompson, her photogenic sons, and Bruce all achieved a modicum of fame from the Fox network's reality show *The Princes of Malibu*. The six-episode show featured the Jenner boys living their privileged life while a grumpy Foster tried to force them to get jobs. Linda, inevitably, would enable the boys to continue their prank-filled lives of freeloading ease. Although much of the on-screen "reality" seemed to be staged, the tension between Linda and David must have been rooted in truth as the two divorced the same year that the show aired.

"The Princes of Malibu," while not a hit, did remind audiences that Linda had once been romantically linked with Elvis, and it sparked an interest in the Jenner family that would grow into the "Keeping Up with the Kardashians" phenomenon. Later, in 2015, Bruce and Kris divorced so that Bruce could transition to being a woman and she became known as Caitlyn Jenner.

While building a successful career, Priscilla dated a lot of men, including Richard Gere and Julio Iglesias. In 1978, she entered into a lengthy romance with a model named Mike Edwards but had to break it off when he advanced on Lisa Marie. Eventually, Priscilla would develop a long-term romance with a screenwriter named Marco Antonio Garcia. The pair lived together for more than two decades and had a son in 1987 while Priscilla worked on *Dallas*. The screenwriters simply wrote in a pregnancy story arc for Jenna Wade to accommodate the circumstance. Priscilla and Marco broke up in 2006. Priscilla never forgot the way that Mike Stone made money from selling a lurid article about their relationship, and she had long ago made Garcia sign an agreement to prevent him from writing a book about their time together.

Lisa Marie, the only child of the Twentieth Century's most famous recording artist, converted to Scientology in the 1980's and married the musician Danny Keough in the fall of 1988. A year later, on May 29, she gave birth to a daughter named Riley Keough. Three years after that, on October 21, 1992 Lisa Marie and Danny welcomed a son they named Benjamin Keough. In the spring of 1994, Lisa Marie divorced her husband. Less than three weeks later she married the only other man of the century who could rival her father's popular musical success: Michael Jackson.

Michael Jackson hailed from one of the poorest areas of the country, Gary, Indiana, where he'd been born in 1958. In the 1960's and 1970's, Jackson gained fame as the youngest and most charismatic member of the musical group, the Jackson 5, that he sang in with his brothers. In 1982, Michael Jackson released his sixth album, *Thriller* which topped the Billboard charts for thirty-seven weeks and featured, along with the title track, all-time hits such as "Billie Jean" and "Beat It."

Thriller made Jackson a star with the status that Elvis Presley had once held, but Jackson was also able to enjoy critical acclaim and won thirteen Grammy awards. That level of stardom, coupled with an unfathomable amount of money, led Jackson to a strange and sequestered life at his Neverland Ranch in California. Over time, Jackson disfigured his face with extreme plastic surgery and was alleged to have hidden relationships with young boys. By the 1990's, audiences gaped at Jackson's light skin, thin nose, and erratic mannerisms the way they once had at Elvis' weight gain and slurred speech.

Lisa Marie had known Jackson since she was a child, but their romance only developed as her marriage to Dannie faltered. In the early 1990's, Jackson faced a series of child-molestation accusations and some thought he married Lisa Marie only to provide a public façade of normalcy. The two remained married for only two years, with Lisa Marie forced to endure Jackson's drug abuse and abject weirdness.

In 2002, Lisa Marie married the melodramatic actor Nicolas Cage, who was an obsessive fan of Elvis Presley. The marriage lasted only four months.

Lisa Marie enjoyed modest success as a recording artist in the early 2000's but eventually retreated from public life while living in an English castle close to a Scientology center. Her son, Benjamin, struggled with drug abuse and committed suicide in 2020. Lisa Marie never recovered from the grief and increasingly used pills to flatten her emotions. Just fifty-four years old, she died on January 12, 2023 from scar tissue that had built up on her bowels as a result of bariatric weight-loss surgery.

Riley Keough started modeling in 2005, as a fifteen-year-old, and turned to acting soon thereafter. In 2010, appropriately enough, she played a musician in the film *The Runaways* which was about the notorious all-girl punk rock band that performed several hits in the 1970's. In 2011, Keough played a prominent part alongside Channing Tatum in the sleeper hit *Magic Mike* about the adventures of a male stripper.

In 2015, Keough played a supporting role in the box-office blockbuster *Mad Max: Fury Road* which received rave reviews from audiences and critics. Since then, Keough developed into one of the busiest and most sought-after actresses in the business, playing dozens of roles in movies and television shows.

In 2015, Keough married an Australian stuntman named Ben Smith Petersen. Riley had been suffering from autoimmune problems due to having contracted Lyme Disease, but she and Ben wanted a child and decided that surrogacy would be the safest route. In August of 2022, the married couple welcomed their baby daughter and named her Tupelo Storm Smith-Petersen. The baby girl is named after the birthplace of her great-grandfather.

After Elvis died, Col. Tom Parker largely exited the public stage. He became heavier, peaking at around three-hundred pounds. He seemed to get control of his gambling addiction when the money started to dry up, but income from his investments allowed him to keep buying Cuban cigars and to enjoy a nice retirement. He reappeared a few times in 1987 to commemorate the tenth anniversary of Elvis' death and in 1993 to celebrate a US postage stamp dedicated to Elvis, but mostly kept to himself. In 1997, a severe stroke downed Parker and he died at the age of 87. The Colonel lived more than twice as long as Elvis Presley.

# Chapter Twenty Nine

# Legacies

Elvis Presley created the idea of the rock star and he also became the first figure to crossover from music to movies in a way that made him the king of all entertainment. The number of books written about Elvis is almost beyond counting. For a few decades after his death, it seemed that everyone who had even the most casual acquaintance with Elvis wrote a memoir about their interactions with the King of Rock n' Roll. Elvis belonged to the culture in a way that no other figure before or since ever has. Like his career, Elvis' legacy has gone through phases, and in the Twenty-First Century, with remakes of his songs hitting number one on the charts and blockbuster biopics about him and Priscilla lighting up big and small screens, he seems as relevant as ever.

During his lifetime, Elvis invited imitation. It was too easy for comedians to curl their upper lip and imitate that distinct southern drawl. As early as 1954, a Texas comic named Carl Nelson (aka "Cheesie") got the locals laughing with his outlandish versions of Elvis' first hit, "That's All Right, Mama." Elvis never minded when someone made a joke about him, and when he met Nelson the two became quick friends and played some songs together for fun.

By 1956, a teenager named Jim Smith learned how to bounce around while imitating Elvis' voice. The impersonation was just good enough to land Smith guest spots on radio and eventually on a lesser-known television variety show. By the 1960's however, a few performers put on Elvis impersonations as a full-time job, touring for audiences at county fairs and local music halls. For fans who would never be able to see the real King, these impersonators offered a chance to enjoy something like the real Elvis experience.

Just before Elvis died, the performance artist/comedian Andy Kaufman created the perfect comic tribute to Elvis. In March of 1977, Kaufman appeared on "The Tonight Show" with Johnny

Paul Smith / Martin Fox / No changes made. Carson. Wearing a suit and Elvis fans still don bedazzled jumpsuits, grease their hair, and swing their hips as impersonators of the King.

tie, Kaufman approached the microphone as a timid man with an undiscernible foreign accent. Then, turning his back to the camera, Kaufman tore the suit off to reveal a black Elvis-style jumpsuit. Kaufman-as-Elvis then combed his hair. After strapping on a guitar, Kaufman performed Elvis' moves to near-perfection and even sang with a melodic southern accent. Audiences loved it. The real Elvis Presley loved it too and said that he thought Kaufman had the best impression of any he'd seen.

In the 1970's, Elvis look-alike contests became a semi-regular feature at bars and clubs around the country. Everyone knew how to imitate Elvis: put on a bedazzled jumpsuit, slick back your hair, curl your lip, say "thank you, very much," and then swivel and karate chop your way through a few iconic songs. Over the decades, everyone from celebrity actors like John Goodman to little-known state politicians like Indiana's Bruce Borders, have gone on-stage to dress and sing like Elvis Presley.

Almost certainly, the most widely viewed Elvis impersonator was the professional wrestler Roy Wayne Harris, who debuted in the World Wrestling Federation (WWF, now known as World Wrestling Entertainment, or WWE) as the Honky Tonk Man in 1986. Although the Honky Tonk Man never explicitly identified as an Elvis impersonator, the sideburns, greasy hair, and sequined jumpsuits left no doubt about who Harris was styling himself after. The Honky Tonk Man would often wow audiences with his swiveling hips, just before cracking opponents upside the head with his guitar as a finishing move.

Movies about Elvis appeared almost immediately after the singer's death. First, there was a 1979 television movie titled *Elvis*. Kurt Russell, who had made his acting debut as a child in the 1963 Elvis picture *It Happened at the World's Fair* now played Elvis Presley himself. Two years later, in 1981, NBC aired its own made-for-television movie titled *Elvis and the Beauty Queen*. In that movie, which was about the love affair between Elvis and Linda Thompson, Don Johnson (of later Miami Vice fame) played Elvis and Stephanie Zimbalist (of Remington Steel fame) played Linda Thompson.

In 2017, a documentary about Elvis titled *The King* debuted at the Cannes film festival and chronicled the life and times of Elvis. Well-produced and nostalgic, *The King* nonetheless reached only a limited audience. In 2018, HBO Films produced a biographical documentary titled *Elvis Presley: The Searcher*. The documentary, suggested by Priscilla, featured Elvis' life story as told through his music. Priscilla presented Elvis as a free spirit in search of universal truths. Fans received the documentary warmly, and Priscilla's involvement indicated her continuing affection for her long-deceased ex-husband.

Most curiously, two comedies have been made about the meeting between Elvis and Richard Nixon. The photo of the two shaking hands, Nixon in a suit and Elvis in a cape, has long been the single most requested photo from the national historical archives in Washington DC and stands as a cultural oddity. In 1997, a movie titled *Elvis Meets Nixon*, with little-known actor Rick Peters playing Elvis, and a character actor named Bob Gunton playing Nixon debuted on cable through the Showtime network as a fake and funny documentary.

Nearly twenty years later, in 2016, Hollywood decided to make a higher production movie about the meeting between the King of Rock n' Roll and the President of the United States. *Elvis and Nixon* featured Michael Shannon as Elvis Presley and Kevin Spacey as

Richard Nixon. The movie captured all the glorious weirdness of the meeting between the two most caricatured and imitated Americans of the Twentieth Century. The movie did not make much money, but most of the critics who saw the film found it to be amusing.

In 2022, Elvis' biography finally received the big-budget Hollywood treatment in the biopic *Elvis* starring Austin Butler as the King. Filming was interrupted by the 2020 covid pandemic, and Butler supposedly spent three years in character as Elvis to prepare for the film. Tom Hanks, who might be described as Elvis' most famous fan (in 2000's Castaway, Hanks played an Elvis-obsessed Fedex pilot) played Col. Tom Parker, who narrates the film. Olivia Dejonge played Priscilla.

*Elvis* the movie managed to encapsulate the raucous life of Elvis Presley, but caused controversy through the use of slick anachronisms (modern rap music in the soundtrack) and what some people considered a glossing over of problems with the romance between Priscilla and Elvis. Col. Tom Parker's alleged involvement in the murder of a woman in Denmark, though well-known by the time of the filming, never gets  mentioned in the film. Still, critics and audiences largely praised Elvis and found the film to be entertaining.

In some ways, the film *Priscilla*, directed by Sophia Ford Coppola served as a counterpoint to the big-budget biopic of Elvis directed by Tom Hanks. Coming in 2023, just a year after *Elvis*, *Priscilla* is a quieter film based on Priscilla Presley's 1985 memoir about her time with Elvis. The film featured the highly respected young actress Cailie Spaeny as Priscilla and focused only on Priscilla's life during her relationship with Elvis (played by the Australian actor, Jacob Elordi). Thus, the film began in 1959 when Elvis met Priscilla in Germany and ended in 1973 when Priscilla left Graceland to pursue a more independent life.

While Coppola's film stopped short of demonizing Elvis, it did force audiences to confront the more uncomfortable aspects of Elvis' relationship with Priscilla that the Tom Hanks film glossed over. Elvis could be controlling, unfaithful, and emotionally unavailable. The ten-year difference that existed between Elvis

In March of 2006, Graceland was made a National Historic Landmark. Every year, more than 500,000 visitors travel to tour the house, grounds, and even Elvis' private aircrafts.

and Priscilla seemed much more pronounced, and unforgivable, at the beginning of the relationship. One scene from the movie, where star-struck nuns at Priscilla's Catholic high school flirted with Elvis as he waited for Priscilla in the school parking lot, demonstrated the power of the King's overwhelming celebrity to erase any faults. What teenage girl, went the thinking, wouldn't want to date Elvis Presley?

Yet, Coppola recognized that Priscilla Presley needed to have a primary voice in her own life's story and Priscilla, while recognizing the problems inherent to her relationship with Elvis, refuses to be defined as a victim. For Elvis Presley to be featured in two major films, forty-five years after his death, indicates the public's ongoing fascination with the King of Rock n' Roll.

Not long after the tragic death of Lisa Marie Presley, the public nearly lost access to Graceland as a company tried to foreclose on the property. After her mother's death, Riley Keough controlled the property and had to file a lawsuit to prevent Graceland from being sold away from her family's possession. A Tennessee judge quickly put a stop to the foreclosure, but the controversy caused panic to the tourist-trade businesses in Memphis and drew attention to a home that has become iconic to generations of Elvis fans. Elvis, as a musician, actor, and eternal brand, lives on into the Twentieth Century as a significant media presence.

The Fall of 2024 saw the publication of Lisa Marie's posthumous memoir. As had been the case with her father, Lisa Marie's life was remarkable, tragic, and defined by the untimely death of a parent. In the same way that Elvis never recovered from the death of his own mother, Lisa Marie spent her adolescent and young adult years coming to terms with the tragedy of her father's passing. After her own son, Ben, died by suicide Lisa Marie's mental health seemed to unravel. As has always been the case with the Presley family, the press quickly turned tragic details about Lisa Marie's response to her son's death into tabloid fodder. The truth seems to be that Lisa Marie loved her own son, Ben, in the same way that Elvis once loved his only child Lisa Marie, and the same way that Gladys had once loved Elvis. Emotions of such strength sing with force that demands the world's attention. Every sad song is preceded by a love song.

Musically, Elvis Presley lives on in countless ways. After rap music dominated black culture in the 1990's, a rapper named Eminem released an LP in 1999 that made him the first white superstar in a traditionally black musical genre. After becoming a success, Eminem would often refer to the parallels between himself and Elvis. Like Elvis, Eminem would have his greatest success with a movie-soundtrack combination in the form of 2001's *Eight Mile.*

In the Twenty-First Century, however, no artist has followed the career trajectory of Elvis more closely than Britney Spears. Like Elvis, Spears debuted as a teenager dancing suggestively. Her album *Baby One More Time...* was coupled with a music video featuring Spears in a barely-there schoolgirl outfit. In 2003, Britney starred in a movie titled *Crossroads.* For the next decade, Britney's life played out in the public sphere as she navigated a failed marriage, motherhood, and a mental health crisis. In 2007, when she danced in a revealing outfit at the Video Music Awards, audiences reacted with shock and derision over the fact that she had gained a few pounds.

Like Elvis, Britney entered middle age by performing at a doomed-from-the-beginning residency in Las Vegas. Also like Elvis, Britney finds her finances controlled by others, and frequently seems sequestered in a vast mansion, surrounded by people who enable her delusions. Fame and fortune, especially when visited upon the very young, does seem to bring about a certain pattern.

The music of Elvis Presley continued to break into the Billboard Music Top 100 even in the Twenty-First Century. A 2001 remake of a Frank-Sinatra film about a criminal caper in Vegas, titled Ocean's Eleven, included a remix of the 1968 Elvis hit "A Little Less Conversation." The remix infused the original song with some upbeat back-music. When released as a single in 2002, it topped the charts in the United Kingdom. Elvis Presley, dead for more than two decades, was still winning new fans.

## About the Author

Dr. Chris Edwards teaches history and English at a public high school in the Midwest. He is a former research affiliate with MIT, a frequent contributor to *Skeptic* magazine, and his original "Connect-the-Dots" teaching method has been published by the National Council for Social Studies and by Rowman and Littlefield Education. He has written several titles for Blue River Press, including *All About the Moon Landing*. Chris is also an educational consultant and is available to give lectures and book signings. He can be reached at scientechsummer@gmail.com.

# From Chris Edwards & Blue River Press
ILLUSTRATED EARLY READER SERIES / GRADES 4 THRU 8

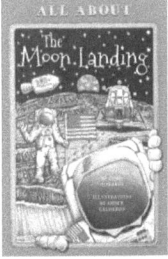

All About the Moon Landing
(9781681571393) 128 pages | $7.99
Amid turbulent times America joined the space race in
a sprint to the Moon. Uncover surprising events and
reflect on the lasting effects of the momentous Moon
Landing and peek into the future of space exploration.

All About Stephen Hawking, 2nd Ed.
(9781681572086) 128 pages | $6.99
Stephen Hawking was diagnosed with ALS at the age
of twenty-one. Hawking didn't let that stop him from
expanding humanities understanding of the scientific
origin of the universe and black holes. This book
covers Hawking's entire life.

All About Helen Keller
(9781681570969) 128 pages | $5.99
This book explores all aspects of Helen Keller life.
From becoming deaf and blind as a toddler to an
effective and world famous advocate for the blind and
women's suffrage. This book covers Keller's entire
life.

# References

Guralnick, P. (1994). Last train to Memphis: The rise of Elvis Presley. Little, Brown and Company.

Nash, Alanna. (2003). The Colonel: The extraordinary story of Colonel Tom Parker and Elvis Presley. Simon and Schuster.

Presley, P., & Edwards, S. (1985). Elvis and me. Berkley Books.

Stanley, D., & Coffey, D. (1993). Elvis: We love you tender. St. Martin's Press.

West, R., West, S., & Hebler, D. (1977). Elvis: What happened? Ballantine Books.